D0583283

Panic Among the Philistines

Panic Among the Philistines

Bryan F. Griffin

Regnery Gateway
Chicago

Copyright © 1983 by Bryan F. Griffin. All rights reserved.

No part of this book may be reproduced in any form or by any electronic or mechanical means, including information storage and retrieval systems, without permission in writing from the publisher, except by a reviewer, who may quote brief passages in a review.

Published by Regnery Gateway, Inc.
360 West Superior Street
Chicago, Illinois 60610-0890

Portions of this book originally appeared in *Harper's* Magazine in different form. Portions of Chapter 18 are reprinted by permission of *The Yale Literary Magazine* from Volume 149, Number 4.

International Standard Book Number: 0-89526-633-4

Library of Congress Cataloging in Publication Data

Griffin, Bryan F.,
    Panic among the philistines.

    1. Literature and society—United States. 2. American literature—20th century—History and criticism.
3. Arts and society—United States. I. Title.
PN51.G74   1983   810'.9'0054   82-60663
ISBN 0-89526-633-4

Manufactured in the United States of America.

In my heterodox heart there is yearly growing up the strangest, crabbed, one-sided persuasion, that *art* is but a reminiscence now; that for us in these days prophecy (well understood), not poetry, is the thing wanted. How can we *sing* and *paint* when we do not yet *believe* and *see*? There is some considerable truth in this; how much I have not yet fixed. Now, what, under such point of view, is all existing art and study of art?

Thomas Carlyle, in a letter to
his brother; October 1, 1833

CONTENTS

Chapter I

The Panic

It was the chilly autumn of 1980, and what was left of the American cultural community had fallen on hard times. Old façades were suddenly crumbling, older masks were finally rotting, and everywhere there was the unspoken fear that the game might soon be up. A few grim-faced defenders of the status quo were arming themselves with faded copies of *Rolling Stone* and swearing that the enemy would get his big ugly attitude slapped before it was all over, but even these brave hearts lacked conviction, probably because nobody could figure out just who the enemy was, exactly, let alone what he looked like or where he was coming from.

One anxious critic from *Time* magazine blamed all the trouble on a small but vicious band of literary "purists," but the *Washington Post* nursed darker

1

visions: "post-romantic inverse snobbery attached to sales figures," muttered one of the *Post*'s book reviewers, and we all shuddered, as we always do when the sales figures are in danger. And indeed, most of the community elders were doing their damnedest to apprehend the threat as they had previously comprehended art, in terms of economic and political trends: "A period of conservatism appears to lie ahead in the arts," warned a former director of the Metropolitan Museum of Art, just back from the front. His name was Thomas Hoving, and he had been to the board rooms of America's artistic institutions to look for some "new blood," as he called it, but he had stumbled into an enemy ambush instead: "Wealthy, old-money, upper-class people with frozen-in-amber attitudes," gasped the white-faced survivor, trying to forget the horrible sight, but knowing that it would be with him for the rest of his days.

He didn't have to say another word: it was common knowledge within the community that educated people with spare cash shouldn't be permitted to have anything to do with art in a democracy, and for years everybody had been planning for the day when teams of poverty-stricken adolescents with determinedly liquid values would be rounded up and forced to administer the nation's cultural institutions. (With the help of some of that divine New Money, apparently: Mr. Hoving was a "cultural consultant," of all things, and for understandable reasons he couldn't help wishing that "arts institutions" would be just a bit more "business-like.") And now suddenly the future was threatening: "You tend to get certain conservative attitudes when you have hard times," said Mr. Hoving darkly, peering through his cultural field glasses at the bloody hills above; which was absolute nonsense, historically, but it made some of the chaps in the bunker feel a little better, because it sounded like behaviorism, instead of art.

Mr. Hoving was and is a sharp and decent man, but also something of an artistic and intellectual neutralist: the really important thing, in his eyes, was to avert a panic. "A lot of people argue that the arts are in crisis," he laughed, trying to sound calm. "I wouldn't agree. Artists and people involved in the administration of the arts are always screaming about crises."

It might have been the voice of appeasement, but it drew some half-hearted applause from an almost forgotten corner of the nation's faculty lounge, where a fifty-year-old professor of creative writing named John Barth was still trying to persuade himself and the *New York Times Book Review* that everything was going to be all right. Like all fifty-year-old professors of creative writing, Mr. Barth was the author of a stack of very long and very precious "innovative" novels, and so naturally he was an old hand when it came to cultural trend-spotting. He was able to say without fear of contradiction that the troubles of 1980 were only temporary, a brief "trend of the decade," and he had it on very good authority that the troops would be home by Christmas: after all, "a culture's trends are not necessarily its monuments," explained the professor, inadvertently leveling most of the artistic reputations on campus, including one very close to his own innovative heart. Closing his eyes to the carnage, Mr. Barth hurried on to apply an eccentric twist to the Hoving thesis: there was indeed a "general conservative reaction," he said, but it was actually a reaction to an exotic academic activity known as "convention-busting," which had been Mr. Barth's particular specialty, in palmier days. And now that he came to think of it, it *was* rather lonely on campus, all of a sudden: not at all like the dear dead days of the glorious 1960s, when "perhaps half" of the kids in the professor's graduate-level seminars in Convention Busting had been feverishly "involved in formally innovative writing of one sort or another." Why, in 1980, "virtually no one was." It must have something to do with the economy, the professor was sure of it: it was all connected in some way with "literary Howard Jarvises," it was a "Proposition-13 mentality" directed against something called "post-modernism," it was...it was...oh my God it was "Reagan Country"!

The full force of Mr. Barth's socioeconomic revelations hit home with a terrifying mental thud: there were shadowy economic moralists abroad in the national quad, and they were "in the ascendancy," and they had made all the Formally Innovative graduate students grow up and go away, and now the moralists were "preaching the family novel" at Mr. Barth, and pretty soon there was going to be a chilling "return to traditional literary values"! Oh it was awful awful it was awful: "The decade of the Moral Majority," whispered the horrified professor, "will doubtless be the decade of"—you could have heard a trend drop—"Moral Fiction." The ghastly vision was complete, and the cries of endangered influence filled the air. Nobody in the faculty lounge was quite sure what a Traditional Literary Value *was*, of course, let alone how to write the filthy stuff, but the whole thing sounded absolutely sick-making. Poor Mr. Barth tried to restore some order to the scene by singing an old 1960s convention-busting lullaby called "Reagan Country is not the whole of Western civilization," but he could hardly hear himself croon: his bizarre literary meditations had aroused far too many defenseless imaginations, and the American cultural campus was in an unholy uproar.

As so often before, some of the most wrenching noises seemed to be coming from another fifty-year-old professor of creative writing named Edgar Doctorow. Mr. Doctorow, a popular writer of rather smutty political novels, was explaining to Victor Navasky of the *Nation* that the increasing legions who were making fun of his scatological tracts were actually "making political judgements in the guise of esthetic objectivity." For obvious reasons, he didn't think that people should be allowed to discuss his literary merchandise in terms of its intellectual or philosophical content: why, "they want to set up a Commissar in the Republic of Letters," howled Mr. Doctorow, as he began to discern the shape of reviews to come.

The mystifying suggestion drew a few well-practiced oohs and ahs from Mr. Navasky, but even he might have admitted that Mr. Doctorow's performance wasn't half as scary as the new show over at *Time* magazine, where a Senior Writer named Frank Trippett was packing the assistant professors in with a gory little piece of innovative writing called "The Growing Battle of the Books." Mr. Trippett had memorized all the relevant political theories, and he seemed to understand that the crisis

involved literature and art in some way, but he'd managed to get the politics and the art all mixed up with
Censorship and—inevitably—Lust.

He had just been handed a field report by a professor
from Indiana University who had actually seen an
enemy regiment, said Mr. Trippett excitedly. The con-
quering purists were being led by parents and teachers
and members of the nation's school boards, many of
whom were "voluntary censors," intent on protecting
everybody from "ugly words, sedition, blasphemy,
[and] unwelcome ideas," which were apparently the
very things that made life worth living, over at *Time*
magazine. This nationwide "populist censorial spirit"
had somehow "sneaked up on the nation," according to
Mr. Trippett; but since nobody could figure out just
how the nation had managed to sneak up on itself, it
was generally agreed that Mr. Trippett had probably
meant to say that the nation had sneaked up on *Time*
magazine, or anyway on Mr. Trippett. In any case, the
flustered Writer had been told (by the President of the
American Library Association, of course) that the con-
querors were "moved" by a warped desire to exercise
"some control over what is close to their lives," and,
being the very model of a modern Senior Writer, he
understood this to mean that they nursed a "hunger for
some power over something," presumably their children. All in all, Mr. Trippett just didn't have much
hope for the future, what with kids in Idaho and Long
Island missing out on Sedition and Blasphemy and
Ugly Words and all: "mind control" was coming, make
no mistake about it. On top of everything else—"and
perhaps worst of all"—the invading patricians were

bent on protecting the schoolchildren from an old chestnut called "reality," in direct defiance of Mr. Trippett's wishes.

Now, it was a funny thing, but back in 1980, people who complained obsessively that the rest of the world wasn't paying enough attention to their private version of "reality" almost always turned out to be talking about sex, and Mr. Trippett was no exception: "Americans [for which read "Frank Trippett and friends"] are in no danger of being pushed back to the prudery of the 19th century," said the Senior Writer hopefully, trying to keep a stiff upper lip about the whole thing, but giving away just a bit more of himself than he'd intended. (It was no coincidence that his sobs harmonized so sweetly with those emanating from the editorial offices of the pornographic magazine *Hustler*, where the guys were also trying to "deal in a realistic world and mirror the reality of the '80s.")

In those days, Senior Writers in New York who couldn't get to sleep at night because children in Idaho Falls weren't being exposed to sufficiently erotic "realities" were almost always the same Senior Writers who imagined that there was more reality in the cinemas of Newark or in the science fiction stories of Kurt Vonnegut than there was in the schoolrooms of Idaho. Ladies and gentlemen of increasingly narrow experience, they were no longer able to see that a parochial "fact" that they'd come across in a Woody Allen film or a Ken Kesey novel was not necessarily an ineluctable reality, or even a particularly interesting truth. And so it was with Mr. Trippett, who found his own pet dreams of reality exactly where one would have expected him to find them, in twentieth-century bestsellers like *Slaugh-ter-House Five, Soul On Ice, Brave New World, Catch-22, One Flew Over the Cuckoo's Nest,* etc.—you know, all the really heavy stuff that would make "a nice library" for "anybody with broad-gauged taste." The determinedly broad-gauged Senior Writer also claimed to be severely frightened by "protests" against *The Merchant of Venice* and *Little Black Sambo,* but he stopped short of calling for a constitutional amendment to prohibit literary protest.

Still, for murky reasons best known to himself, Mr. Trippett was exceedingly anxious to ensure that all school boards and librarians be required to approve his personal 1960s reading list for study in the country's 1980 schools. Not surprisingly, his efforts to halt the social clock were being happily ignored all over the continent, and accordingly the danger was "ubiqui-tous." Somehow Mr. Trippett had found out about a little library in a small town in North Carolina, for instance, a library that wouldn't let children borrow adult books without permission, and the spectre positively scared the editorial pants off him. Children in Whiteville, North Carolina, growing up sans Vonne-gut, sans Cleaver, sans Kesey, sans *reality?* The prospect just didn't bear thinking about. And then there was the satanic schoolboard in Anaheim that had insolently issued a list of approved classroom texts that did not include "some previously studied books" that were especial favorites of Mr. Trippett's. Why it was intoler-able! What was *happening* to the world? Had everybody but Mr. Trippett gone crazy? The modern Senior Writer grew more excited with each new atrocity story, and pretty soon he was waving his literary hands in the air and being reminded—ever so forcefully—of an all-purpose ghost story called "The Rise of Adolph Hitler's Germany."

What he was also being, of course, was pretty silly; but it was exactly the sort of silliness that his audience had been hoping to see, and a thrilling time was had by all. After all, it was much better for one's cultural image to be seen cowering at the memory of Nazi Germany, than to be seen cowering in the face of democratic Whiteville, North Carolina. And Mr. Trippett was quite right to be a little nervous: as more and more parents and teachers and school boards and librarians and booksellers began to remove more and more obsolete cult novels from more and more crowded shelves and reading lists, the Frank Trippetts of the community were going to grow more and more lonely. The prospect of cultural isolation is rarely a cheerful one, and even Senior Writers like a bit of company; indeed, what the last of the old guard wanted most of all was merely someone to hold their collective hand, someone to tell them that there were still other people who saw the same sad visions they had seen, someone to reassure them that their lost world had been "real," too. And if, towards the end, that reassurance had to be extracted almost forcibly from a covey of innocent thirteen-year-olds in Idaho Falls or Whiteville, North Carolina, well, it was better than nothing.

Trying to keep one shaking toe in the real world, the troubled Trippett did concede that he wasn't *really* all that worried about the threat of "official monitoring": he was worried about something brand new called "popular censorship," which was a phrase he'd made up to describe the new mood in the rest of the country. The most terrifying manifestation of "popular censorship" was a thing called "closet censorship," which was what happened when the parents and teachers and librarians decided—without permission from *Time's* Board of Permissible Reality—that the nation's children needn't read what Mr. Trippett wanted the nation's children to read. That's how it always works, of course: first comes the private editorial line to the one true "reality," and then there's the growing certainty that Senior Writers on the East Coast are *much* more qualified than the teachers and parents and librarians of Idaho to decide what the children of Idaho should be studying, and then it's only a matter of time before the editorial guardians of Reality are ready to enforce their personal "reality" fantasies on their fellow citizens, and on children in particular. The editorial hysteria sets in when the citizens and their children begin to grow bored with the editorial fantasy; then are there enemy commandos seen behind every cultural trend and every suburban school board, then is the night filled with the anguished cries of "censorship" and "mind control."

Mr. Trippett gave the game away when he said he'd heard tell of an enemy officer—a member of an Indiana school board, of course—who'd said that "the bottom line" was "who will control the minds of the students." For obvious reasons, this was a bit too blatant for Mr. Trippett. The poor Senior Writer might have been hopelessly confused about the meanings of big aristocratic words like "censorship" and "reality" and "literature," but one thing was horribly horribly clear: a cultural hierarchy that was beginning to lose its grip on the minds and hearts of the younger generations was a cultural hierarchy heading for a crash. The "resurgent moralistic mood" was No Laughing Matter, and Cotton Trippett was personally going to make damn sure that it got stamped out before some poor kid got moral, or even literate.

But if cultural reactionaries like the Trippetts and the Doctorows and the Barths were almost embarrassingly eager to define the threat in political terms, more sophisticated victims were proposing more sophisticated enemies. The fiercely modern theatrical producer Joseph Papp, for example, had noticed a lot of old plays around town lately, and he was getting nervous: it was "sentimentality," that's what it was, sentimentality—and sentimentality was "decadent." "People want the good old days back," complained the sixty-year-old showman, sounding just a bit bewildered by the sudden turn of events. He himself would never be associated with a "revival," of course, because all revivals were "out of date," and Mr. Papp was Never Ever Out Of Date, please God: "*I* wouldn't do it," he declared wistfully. The up-to-date producer stood around looking unsentimental for a while, and then wandered off to produce a revival of *The Pirates of Penzance,* apparently under the impression that Gilbert and Sullivan were a couple of young sax players from Nutley. "Who am I to be a wet blanket about anything that brings people to the theatre?" he muttered somewhat sheepishly, trying to keep at least one finger in every camp, and succeeding.

But even as Mr. Papp was endeavoring to get a fix on the most elusive trend he'd ever seen, Truman Capote was drifting through the corridors of art saying that it was No use, no use: the enemy wasn't "sentimentality" at all, the enemy was Jealousy. The stout-hearted little trooper was still trying to smile bravely, but he was pretty sure he'd heard a sudden explosion of "envy" during the night: "People simply cannot *endure* success," explained Mr. Capote, and so naturally the people—those notorious literary purists—were bent on "destroying" Mr. Capote and all his good works.

Before long the condemned man was joined on the block by the literary sexologist Gay Talese, who was telling the *Washington Post* and anyone else he could find that his latest book had made all the literary critics "unhappy" and "vengeful," and inspired in them an unholy "desire to destroy." And it wasn't your run-of-the-mill vengefulness, either: "[It's] a desire to destroy *me*," boasted Mr. Talese, elbowing Mr. Capote's feeble martyrdom aside. "I've done that, or the book has done it, or the both of us have done it." Mr. Talese regarded himself as "likable," why shucks he had *always* been enormously "well-liked," but now all that was "changing": "People who don't know me are angry with me" said the saddest boy in town. There was "venom" in the air, there was "meanness" in the breeze. There was a bottomless "depth of anger" everywhere you looked, and all of human nature was suddenly "mean-spirited" and "ugly." "The response to me has not been pleasant," concluded the proud victim, beating his theme into the ground with uncharacteristic restraint.

By this time the hysteria had spread across all social

and disciplinary boundaries, and nobody was too terribly surprised when Pauline Kael of the *New Yorker* suddenly scrambled out of her cinematic foxhole and took out after the new generation of moviegoers. Ms. Kael was mad as hell because some of the new kids were beginning to stay away in droves from the films that Ms. Kael was telling them to go see, the really fun films that would "tie up their guts" and "give them nightmares." Ms. Kael *never* allowed herself to be seen in public with untied guts; indeed, she'd always thought that the really kicky thing about the Talkies was that they gave one a chance to "experience a sense of danger," right there in the middle of a great big city, and if the new sissies thought there was something a little weird about that, if they thought they were being "more discriminating" by running away from the yummy "sight of blood," well, Ms. Kael was there to tell them that she wasn't about to give up quietly.

And she didn't. In later years, students of Pauline Kael's most psychologically revealing moments would recall with a certain fondness the day the two-fisted lady went to see a film accurately described by the critic Judith Martin as "coy and unappetizing pornography." The meal in question consisted of "two hours of pictures of youths raping one another, committing crimes ranging from purse-snatching to cold-blooded murder, suffering official brutality, and getting stoned," and there were lingering close-ups of "the pain of a child's being sodomized," the "mean face of a prostitute as she sits on the toilet and invites a child to observe the bloody body of a fetus she has just aborted," and other scenes of sadomasochism calculated to appeal to certain unhappy moviegoers. Our Ms. Kael *adored* it: why, it was "good enough to touch greatness," she sighed, alone now in her solitary pleasures; and what's more "it restores your excitement about the confusing pleasures that movies can give." Such comments are better left alone, to stand by themselves.

But all that was in the future. At the moment Ms. Kael was still too furious to sigh about anything. Kids these days had too much "good taste," that's what it was: "Delicacy is once again becoming a mark of culture and breeding," cried the sixty-year-old daredevil, spreading the warning to every Westchester village and town. It wasn't long before Ms. Kael's bizarre theories of violence began to get all wound up with her thoughts about Lust In The Back Row, and the results were just a tad embarrassing: "Squeamishness—surely with terror and prurient churnings under it?—is the basis of this good taste," she sneered, just daring anyone to accuse her of prurient squeamishness. Nobody knew quite what she had in mind, but the ragged troops gave her one last weary cheer for having aligned herself foursquare against Delicacy, Discrimination, Breeding, and Good Taste, the Four Horsemen of the Cultural Apocalypse.

In the end, though, the age-old complaint of the hunted Philistine sounded most pitiably from the lips of schlock novelist John ("Garp") Irving, who was peering nervously under all the literary beds and explaining to anybody who would listen that the forces of "elitism" and "snobbishness" were out to get him. "People in the literary community who have enough money and reputation should be careful not to sneer at the notion that other serious writers might also want enough money and reputation," pouted Mr. Irving, the recipient of writing grants from the Rockefeller Foundation, the Guggenheim Foundation, and the National Endowment for the Arts. The Elitists and the Snobs were cold and ruthless, and all of a sudden they were everywhere: "I'm distressed to hear how many people in the literary community seem to frown on commercial success," wailed the man of the people, and the frightening implication was that two horrible street gangs from the nineteenth century were going to tie Mr. Irving up and make faces at him until, God forbid, his own sales figures started plummeting.

Oh, it was a scary time to be alive! Everybody was pointing the trembling finger at everybody else, but nobody knew just what to do, or where to hide: the impertinent winds of change were howling again, and there was stark terror down amid the Manhattans and the Vodka Sours.

Chapter II

As We Were

The collapse had come with astonishing speed, or so it seemed to the victims. Less than a decade earlier, at the start of the 1970s, the political novelist William Styron had been able to say with a straight face that his generation of intellectuals was putting up "a pretty good show," culturally speaking. He was especially proud of the professional creative writers of his time: "Whether or not we shall receive posterity's sweet kiss," he said coyly, "it has been a rich time for writing, I think, richer than may be imagined." He told *Esquire* magazine that he was thinking of guys like "Mailer, Baldwin, Jones, Capote, Salinger." Also "Gore Vidal, John Barth, Terry Southern, Heller, Walker Percy, Peter Matthiessen." Not to mention "William Gaddis, Richard Yates, Evan Connell, George Mandel, Herbert Gold, Jack Kerouac, Vance Bourjaily, John Clellon Holmes, Calder

16

Willingham, Alan Harrington, John Phillips, William Gass, and, honorifically, George Plimpton." (Mr. Styron had a way of mixing a very little bit of wheat with his chaff, but it was entirely unintentional.)

"No gathering," gulped the novelist modestly, "ever comprised a clutch of talents so remarkably various." As if that weren't enough to stop the conversation dead in its tracks, Mr. Styron went on to declare that "the poets of this generation" would also "sparkle brightly" after Posterity (the old hussy) had kissed them. "From Simpson to Merwin, James Dickey to Anthony Hecht, Snodgrass to Allen Ginsberg," they were all going to sparkle, yes they were, every one of them. Mr. Styron agreed with John Hollander ("himself a fine poet") that the generation of sparklers stood as "some sort of testament" to the "struggle to redeem poetry" from the "sickness with which Literature as a realm is too often infected" (that's the way those guys *wrote*, in the dizzy years). As a matter of fact he thought that his generation was a bit like F. Scott Fitzgerald's, only better, of course. He had been reading an old essay by Fitzgerald, and he had found in it an "odor of death" and a "sense of decline," and such things were foreign to Mr. Styron and his friends: "Writing now at roughly the same age as Fitzgerald, I can say that I feel no such a falling off, no similar sense of loss about my own generation."

And as for Mr. Styron himself, well, watch out, world, he'd "never felt so young." Why, he would not have been at all astonished if "our truly most precious flowering lay in the time to come." The Most Precious Blossom took a deep breath: "Revolution rends the air," he shrieked; "the world around us shivers with the brave racket of men seeking their destiny, with the invigorating noise of history in collision with itself." None of it seemed too terribly relevant, coming from a man who was at that moment working on a play about venereal diseases called "In the Clap Shack," but it had an extraordinarily good beat: "This generation, once so laggardly, now confronts a scene astir with great events, such a wild dynamo of dementedly marvelous transactions that merely to be able to live through them should be cause for jubilation," roared the excited novelist, almost toppling out of his ivory tower. *"Mes amis,"* he howled, *"aux barricades!"*

And then suddenly, less than ten years later, it was all over. Many of the names that had once seemed so glorious to Mr. Styron had been easily forgotten, and most of those that were still remembered had become synonyms for a particularly quaint strain of eccentric mediocrity. Dr. Styron's Wild Dynamo of Demented Transactions was fast becoming a cultural memory, and a rather yawn-making one at that. When Norman Mailer tried to recapture the Spirit of Styron in 1980, he found himself delivering a eulogy instead. "Our prediction is safe," chanted Mr. Mailer, shutting his eyes tight and wishing on a star. "We will break out of our cyst, infiltrate other disciplines, inhabit new epistemological modes. We will exfoliate." There was an awkward pause, and the little cyst-breaker opened one cultural eye. "Excelsior!" he muttered. "I mean, Excalibur!"

It was a sign of the times that nobody bothered to correct him, simply because it didn't seem to matter anymore: an era was dying with bewildering speed, and not all the righteous incantations in the English-speaking world could restore the patient to health. By 1980, even the most persistent apologists for the old regime—the philosophical beneficiaries of the former establishment, the third-generation imitators and the elderly camp followers—had begun to understand that the long party was finally over, and that the giddy era of aberrant art and thought was about to be kicked aside as nothing more than that: one more aberration in the affairs of men, one more futile deviation from the human aim, one more wasted chance, one more century—a crucial one, this time—frittered away by half-souled harlequins disguised as full-hearted heirs of Athens. In its eleventh hour, Western culture had been led up the garden path, and abandoned in the brambles, one more time.

Chapter III

Sudden Exposures

And yea, terror bred confusion, and confusion quickly became panic. Some of the boys and girls who hadn't made it to the lifeboats in time were beginning to run around in circles, trying hard to look like Purists and intellectual Elitists, but nobody could remember what it was *like*, exactly, to be a purist, and in the general chaos some of the slower kids were left standing around without many clothes on at all.

The cult novelist Jerzy Kosinski, for instance, was in an awful state because he seemed to have lost the knack of offending his readers. "My characters insult them, mock their values," insisted Mr. Kosinski. It was a suitably embarrassing psychological revelation, but it didn't go very far towards easing the novelist's growing difficulties: "Just to keep up with inflation, my readers should increase by thirty per cent a year," said the anxious Mocker of Values; "but they don't."

The words were ominous ones, issuing as they did from the lips of the English professor who had slaved for almost twenty years to secure his reputation as the

20

most offensive little grenadier in the literary cellars. Just ten years earlier Mr. Kosinski had been knocking them dead all over Manhattan with evil little fictional atrocities like *The Painted Bird* (an exploration of "every brutality and bestiality man's animal nature is capable of," according to one clear-eyed reviewer) and *Steps*, which received a National Book Award because it dared to go where so many other books had gone before. Most of those who had been tricked into reading *Steps* in 1968 (and who wasn't) had been able to forget its grisly details by 1980, but a reviewer for John Wakeman's *World Authors* was around to jog our memories, with admirable succinctness:

> In *Steps*, an anonymous narrator describes or recalls a series of incidents, most of them sexual, most of them violent, perverse, or grotesque. In one a soldier found cheating in an obscene game has his genitals crushed between bricks; in another a punished child revenges himself on the world by feeding ground glass to his friends; in several others love is exploited or perverted in the pursuit of power, which is itself a tool of hatred. Here, indeed, is just such a world as might have been conceived by the emotionally crippled hero of *The Painted Bird*.

Here indeed was just such a novel as might have been conceived by Jerzy Kosinski, and here too was just the sort of thing calculated to excite the pitter-patter of sheltered little academic hearts all over America. Up at Princeton they decided that Mr. Kosinski was a real must for the English department (not to mention, God help us, the Council for the Humanities), over at Yale they resolved to let him loose for two years in the Drama department (and you wonder why they can't write good plays anymore), and at the American Academy of Arts and Letters they got so giggly that before anybody knew what was happening they'd handed the happy little Humanist a nice warm grant, that he might more easily pursue his unusual literary interests.

And then the world changed. In the early 1980s, Mr. Kosinski was really having to sweat to maintain his rather peculiar reputation as a Mocker of Values and professional "existential cowboy." All of a sudden he was making appearances in existential Hollywood movies and inviting stray journalists up to the office to look at his private collection of photographs of "stunning man-woman figures posing naked." One Canadian film critic reported seeing "illustrated records of free-wheeling sex orgies, carefully lit and orchestrated by Kosinski, miles of flesh unfurled in the thick photo albums he stores in his office." The same observer saw "a large photo" of Mr. Kosinski's "companion of fifteen years" floating "nude on her back in a swimming pool," and listened patiently to Mr. Kosinski's elucidation of the Spirit of Eastern Europe:

> To us sex was the only positive force left in society. Everything else was distracting and dehumanizing.... Every one of us in Poland was preoccupied with it. We rebelled because of it.

And so Mr. Kosinski chattered away in ever more strident tones about his solitary preoccupations, the preoccupations he had ridden to what he had thought were all the best literary parties in town; but even as he passed around the dirty pictures, the light was fading, and the room was growing cold: "Some people think

I'm manipulative and self-centered. They think I'm perverse. There are people who simply would not sit beside me at dinner. They have read my fiction, and it has made them uneasy."

Mr. Kosinski's efforts to convince himself that rampant boredom was really uneasiness constituted a very good try, but his tortured rationalizations could not obscure the awkward fact: the professor had been revealed. Chatter as he might, the Existential Cowboy could no longer disguise the scantiness of his intellectual clothing. It is one of the first rules of the literary game that an armchair shocker can't just sit around and plead his case on the grounds that he once made them swoon in the faculty lounge; he must get up from the table and do some heavy shocking, or the literary party will move on, in search of fresher kicks. Carlyle:

> In general, leave "Literature," the thing called "Literature" at present, to run through its rapid fermentations (how more and more rapid they are in these years!) and to fluff itself off into Nothing, in its own way—like a poor bottle of soda water with the cork sprung;—it won't be long.

Mr. Kosinski's fermentations were rapid enough, but his public discomfort didn't begin to rival that of the "cultural historian" Max Lerner. Mr. Lerner, a former dean of the Graduate School at Brandeis University, was the author of all sorts of big disapproving volumes with titles like *America As A Civilization* and *Education and a Radical Humanism*, and he'd been dispensing moral and literary judgements from the columns of the Civilization's newspapers for more than fifty years—all in all, a most unlikely candidate for public discomfort. But in 1980 he surfaced rather abruptly in the soiled pages of Gay Talese's exhausting survey of sex in fringe America, and to everybody's horror he surfaced smack in the middle of a Californian "sex community."

"On some evenings," recalled Mr. Talese, in his inimitable fashion, "there were gathered around the fireplace, conversing in various stages of dress and sometimes nude, such individuals as," well, such individuals as the guy who wrote *The Joy of Sex*, and the curator of a "museum of erotic art," and a feminist artist who produced "heroic paintings of sexual passion," and...and "the *New York Post*'s syndicated columnist Max Lerner." Max Lerner. Max Lerner! Bill Moyers of the Public Broadcasting Service whirled into action and hurriedly scheduled a two-part television interview with Mr. Lerner so that the grand old theorist could let loose with a few spare moral judgements, but somehow it just wasn't the same anymore. It was, as a matter of fact, more than a little sad; because even though Mr. Lerner was all dressed up in his toughest old work shirt, he looked...he looked as though he weren't wearing anything at all! The English novelist Malcolm Bradbury once said that Mr. Lerner was "less concerned for literature as such than for its expressive function in revealing the culture"; in 1980, many observers were suddenly less concerned for Max Lerner's literature as such than for Max Lerner's expressive function in revealing his own culture.

Not that Mr. Lerner and Mr. Kosinski were alone in assuming new cultural responsibilities during the time of transition. There was the very highly decorated John

Cheever, for instance, who had once been "one of America's major novelists," in the patented phrase of the Book-of-the-Month Club (the organization in charge of mid-level literary titles). Why, it seemed like only the other day that we'd been falling all over one another in the rush to celebrate Mr. Cheever's extended analysis of American masturbatory habits in his novel *Falconer* (the book that had convinced John Gardner that "no one in the world is really good," that had thrilled Robert Towers of the *New York Review* with its "extreme sordidness," that had impressed Janet Groth with its "terrible scenes of cruelty, degradation and lust"); and now all of a sudden here he was, hawking a line of men's watches in the pages of the *New Yorker*. And how awkwardly the mighty had fallen: called up on the mat to explain his unliterary activities, Mr. Cheever tried to sweeten his new image by announcing that he'd never actually *owned* one of the watches before making his decision to appear in the advertisements. But the former Major Novelist couldn't trust himself to talk about it anymore: "I don't believe people should have to explain *everything* they do," huffed the apprentice adman, scrambling to get back into his metaphorical Artist's tweeds before the spotlight went away.

The tweedy part of Mr. Cheever tried to make amends by knocking out a "What I Believe About Art" sort of essay for *Parade* magazine (which was in itself a remarkable concession to tweed, since Cheever-art usually appeared in *Playboy*), and the message was one of desperate hope: "Cretins do indeed write books for one another, but they do not rule the scene," insisted Mr. Cheever, standing up for the community's (and incidentally John Cheever's) sales charts. It was a well-intentioned defense, but somehow the tone was all wrong, especially in the suspension-of-disbelief department: "Literature is produced by a genuinely dedicated group of professionals who hope to be paid enough to educate their children and keep warm in the winter," whispered the plaintive artist, huddling closer to the winking literary embers, and trying to pretend he wasn't the same chap who had once demonstrated his Dedicated Professionalism by filling three consecutive pages with graphic descriptions of various male sexual members ("black, white, red, yellow, lavender, brown," etc.) and by filling ten times as many pages with equally graphic analyses of the intellectual crises of middle-aged American academics ("no girl, no ass, no mouth could get him up"). Anything for the children's education, presumably. Mr. Cheever managed to utter the obligatory words about "our shared knowledge of the power of love and the forces of memory," but even he seemed to realize that it was far too late for another costume change. Most ominous of all was the fact that nobody had said a *word* about *Falconer*, or even asked the Dedicated Professional if he had anything new to say about sexual self-gratification. The damned purists. "I shan't talk about it, I think," muttered Mr. Cheever. He was referring to a line of men's wrist watches, but nobody was listening anymore.

In the Time of Onan

The late John Cheever was not the least attractive

performer of his day (on the contrary, he was a fundamentally decent writer who had composed some very
pleasant short stories in his time), and *Falconer* was not
the most repulsive gatherer of dust on the shelves. If Mr.
Cheever's activities were not causing a great deal of
excitement in 1980, it was not because his occasional
offenses against civility and literature had been too
great, but because they had not been great enough: he
was merely one uneasy soul among many, and his
neighbors had other things to worry about.

Even those members of the *New Yorker*'s staff who
shared the Major Novelist's literary interest in certain
solitary occupations were suddenly very busy with their
own sad thoughts. Gay Talese's good friend Michael
Arlen, for instance, was dashing about the countryside
trying to persuade stray journalists that the act of
watching television was very, "very close to masturbation." Mr. Arlen's revelation had come upon him when
he'd noticed—at the inevitable age of fifty—that television watching was "something somebody does in a
room by oneself in a kind of a daze in a kind of a space of
one's own," or something kind of like that sort of in a
kind of a way. (Ah, that dear old *New Yorker* style!) Mr.
Arlen's own philosophizing was apparently something
that he did in a room by himself in a kind of a daze in a
kind of a space of his own: he was just positive that his
fellow citizens had a "deep connection" to the "unusual
passivity" of the "process" of television watching, and
golly, it was all "rather sexual," though for reasons Mr.
Arlen could not comprehend, his fellow citizens would
"rather not get into that." Mr. Arlen wished that everybody *would* get into that, because Mr. Arlen's lonely

studies had convinced him that the *real* reason that
parents didn't like their children to watch too much
television by themselves was—well, the poor chap
began to get Rather Sexual at that point, and we would
"rather not get into that."

Mr. Arlen is being so cruelly mocked here not because
he disapproved of excessive television watching—he
was of course right to do so—but because he seemed
unable to express his disapproval except in sexual
terms, and in peculiarly adolescent sexual terms at that.
His offenses, like those of Mr. Cheever, were offenses
against manners and logic, but they were also offenses
against a civilization in peril. In the words of an anonymous author of the previous century, the gentlemen
were talking nonsense on the edge of an abyss.

And the cultural authorities at the *New Yorker* had
plenty of intellectual company: in those days, the entire
artistic establishment was "into" Mr. Arlen's euphe-
mistic That. "That" was the spirit that the artist Vito
Acconci—"one of the best-known American avant-
gardists now at work," according to a star-struck child
at the *Washington Post*—was pandering to when he
offered to fondle himself to the point of sexual ecstasy in
the presence of visitors to a SoHo art gallery (a modest
man, Mr. Acconci proposed to be hidden from view
during the actual creative process). And "That" was
what the critic Jim Miller of *Newsweek* was thinking of
when he recommended "a cheerfully raunchy song
about masturbation." And "That" was what Gore
Vidal was talking about when he said that the critic
Edmund Wilson's erotic memoirs were inferior to some
of Mr. Vidal's favorite Victorian pornography, because

"we" didn't know what the Victorians looked like, and such ignorance was "an important aid to masturbation." "I am not sure just why Wilson felt that he should write so much about c—k and c—t," said Mr. Vidal, with puzzled air and characteristic vocabulary (he didn't use dashes; we do): poor Mr. Wilson had not known what Mr. Vidal knew so well, that erotic memoirs were "engaging"—as an "aid to masturbation," presumably—only when the memorialists were "interested in getting laid as often as possible in as many different ways and combinations."

It was not particularly interesting (or surprising) that the fifty-five-year-old Vidal should have allowed himself to ramble on in the manner of Cheever and Arlen (after all, he had just announced that his next book would be published by Lyle Stuart, whose current bestseller was the autobiography of the pornographic-movie star Linda Lovelace); but it was interesting—and indicative—that the editors of the *New York Review of Books* should have seen fit to print and distribute those ramblings. The editors of the *Review* suspected a nasty truth that more serious editors would have found hard to credit: that there was a specialized and literate audience for the onanistic view of human existence and culture, and that this audience was to be found amid the ruins of the shattered cultural hierarchy—among the readers of the *New York Review of Books*. It was an audience left over from the days of Warhol and Morrissey and Hockney and Roth (remember Roth?), an old audience gone gray and gone public.

In less frantic times, the professional narcissists had been more circumspect, decorating their solitary sub-

ject with longer hair and with talk of art and culture;
but the scam had never worked very well. When the
artist David Hockney had had himself filmed back in
1976 taking a "long and meditative douche," and "cuddling up on a sofa with a new boyfriend," the film critic
John Weightman of *Encounter* magazine had fallen for
the decorative chatter, and had therefore been confused
by what he saw. "What has this to do with art," he cried,
"or art history?" Mr. Weightman saw that Mr. Hockney
had closed-circuit television in his bedroom, with the
camera focused on the bed, "as if his most intimate
moments needed reflection to the self," and this was
also most confusing: Why, "a sense of shame is totally
missing," said Mr. Weightman, edging away from the
specialized audience. Pretty soon the screen was pink
with the form of one of Mr. Hockney's old boyfriends
"in active copulation with a third, unidentified young
man," and Mr. Weightman began to catch on: "In the
erotic scene," the critic said thoughtfully, "the two
young men have identically beautiful bodies and (surprise!) grapple, not as one had always thought *more
canino*, but face to face, as if Narcissus had fallen flat on
to his own image and were making love to himself."

Alas, like so many who had glimpsed the truth before
1980, Mr. Weightman was reluctant to express it, lest he
look like an independent thinker, and pretty soon he
was wondering if the "transvestite Miss World Contest
in the middle of the film" was perhaps "not a gratui-
tous fill-in, as I first thought it was, but a relevant piece
of grotesquerie, since its extreme negation of physical
attractiveness brings out the tragedy of beauty,
which"—but never mind. It was a sign of the times that

Mr. Weightman's independence survived only as an obligatory "perhaps": "What the film is suggesting, perhaps, is that in the given world...there can be no stability of the beautiful or acceptability of the non-beautiful. The only relative stability is in the objectification of art—for which the lucky Narcissus is gifted, and the other not."

But that sort of kindly gibberish was beginning to be a thing of the past. By the early 1980s the Hollywood literati had been indulging themselves in certain intellectual perversities for so many years that they had forgotten that perversity must be disguised with loud chants of Redeeming Social Value if it is to be tolerated by the real world. Certain sharp-eyed playwrights and novelists and "film makers" had begun to catch on, and the consequences were no less embarrassing for being inevitable.

An Australian film about life at a Catholic boys' school was a case in point. One of the very few whole-souled film critics in America, Judith Martin of the *Washington Post*, summarized the action:

> Only one aspect of the religious life is shown: the sexual feelings of the monks and their pubescent pupils. Masturbation is Topic A at this establishment, and also B, C, and D.... One monk goes about screaming "I hate life," and "Your body is your worst enemy" and "You must be on guard against all your senses at all times"—and is tortured by erotic dreams. Another, elderly and mellow, argues "What's wrong with masturbation? It has to come out somehow." The little boys go after themselves and one another. Some of them turn to masochism, in rituals that end in one boy's death....

The advertising campaign for this heated little fantasy was aimed at one audience, and at one audience only. The campaign was built around a photograph of a naked youth, framed by enormous black print: "Young men torn between physical desire and religious discipline!" Not a very subtle come-on, perhaps; but more polite in its implications than the line delivered by one poor juvenile actor in the movie: "You'll probably die playing with yourself."

Did it work? Well you bet it did. The gang fell for it without even token resistance, and the boys and girls also fell all over one another in the race for the best seats. Kevin Thomas, *Los Angeles Times*: "Amazingly seductive." David Ansen, *Newsweek*: "Impressive." Judy Stone, *San Francisco Chronicle*: "Daring." Archer Winsten of the *New York Post:* "Brilliantly presents that old problem of male puberty" (ah yes). A bitter reviewer at the *Washington Post*: "A comic odyssey that documents the stirring of a responsive, life-affirming vision from the remains of a misdirected religious impulse" (again, ah yes). A characteristically tiresome butterfly at the *Village Voice* did her duty and said that the director of the fantasy was "Australia's most accomplished director," David Denby of *New York* magazine said that the same guy was, like the rest of his friends, "a major filmmaker," and dear Pauline Kael fell over the edge and called the man "a great filmmaker." None of which was very surprising, since the distributors of the film had been careful to warn the kids that the product had Won Every Major Australian Film Award.

It was Mr. Denby of *New York* who treated spectators

to the most embarrassing performance. The object in question was a "wonderful" movie, in Mr. Denby's wide-open eyes, primarily because "the thirteen-year-old hero" carried the day against "black-cassocked Catholic brothers" (all hiss the black cassocks). "As they preach denial of the flesh," continued Mr. Denby, sounding somewhat agitated in his artistic excitement, "his erection bulges under his clothing." Well you should have *been* there. Before it was all over the overwrought critic had thrown all caution to the winds and could be found sashaying around in the pages of his magazine, clothed only in his stifling resentment: "This young-man's movie is filled with outrage over the suppression of natural instincts." The poor chap began to reminisce about one "extraordinary sequence" in which a monk dreamt he was "swimming naked underwater with four ravishing girls," but we will draw the curtain.

Or rather, we would have liked to draw the curtain. Alas, for obvious reasons that we will not spell out, Mr. Denby's appalling performance attracted the attention of the film's very clever distributors; they grabbed his review and attached it to their national advertisements, just above the nude boy's left buttock—and newspapers around the country proceeded to reprint the awful thing.

Such a move was to be expected, perhaps. For years American newspapers had been only too happy to pander to the republic in all its ghastly "pluralism." Journals like the *New York Times* and the *Chicago Tribune* and the *Washington Post* were celebrating the cultural crash by accepting advertisements for uncompromising films such as *Teenage Fantasies, Ultra Flesh, Dallas School Girls* ("good-looking fresh new faces and bodies"), *Little Girls Blue, Talk Dirty to Me, Screwples, Coed Fever, French Teen, Little Darlings* ("don't let the title fool you"), and *Peppermint Soda* ("the nymphet-watcher in me was shamefully stirred," boasted Andrew Sarris of the *Village Voice*). And if Great Organs Of Opinion like the *Times* and the *Tribune* and the *Post* were more than eager to act as pimps for films that aimed to entertain solitary admirers of very young female flesh, why should they refuse to carry advertisements for films that had been made for literary worshippers of Onan? If the *Post*, for example, didn't draw the line at reprinting leering come-on quotations from *Screw* magazine ("the sex scenes are incredibly well paced") or *Hustler* ("incredibly erotic," "earns a masters degree in erotica") or *Elite* ("high-powered erotic action") or *Swank* ("will bring out the bull in you") or *High Society* ("probing explicitly the kinkiness of the rich," "by far the best porno film of the decade"), how could it be expected to draw the line at Mr. Denby's more pitiful meanderings? Why should a paper that made a regular practice of interviewing like-minded "sex therapists" ("he advises a variety of techniques, ranging from deep breathing...to masturbation") draw the line at anything, if there was money in it, and if it could be propped up with vague whispers about the First Amendment and "reality"?

Cultural sickness—and an unchecked obsession is a sickness—always leads to individual tragedy. It was only a matter of time before a heavy thinker from *Artforum* magazine found himself musing about the epistemological purposes of a "body artist" who had "proceeded inch by inch to amputate his own penis, while a photographer recorded that art event." The critic was pretty sure that all modern artists were merely trying, in their own inimitable fashion, to "re-interpret the Leonardian knowing-how-to-see in post-Euclidean terms," and he, for one, was Proud To Be Living In A Free Country: "In advanced capitalist countries, the intelligentsia has sufficient self-confidence for its purveyors of cultural goods to include Earthworks and bodyworks in their inventories." In those days, the "intelligentsia" included (a) the guy who held that bloody camera, and (b) certain philosophers at *Artforum* magazine. The villain in the piece was not of course the miserable wretch who committed the mad act—he is not really a fit subject for ridicule—but the perversion of thought that suggested the atrocity to him in the first place, and that welcomed it as a fit subject for art criticism. The irony was that the Body Artist had gone too far with the popular obsession: he had cut himself off from the only thing worth talking about. He had divorced himself from his artistic sensibility, so to speak, and isolated himself from the rest of the cultural establishment.

But then, isolation was the theme of the age: it was a time of self-absorption, in more ways than one. It was left to John Leonard of the *New York Times* to sum up the intellectual context of the moment, as he brought his increasingly common sensibility to bear on a perfectly rational book about Oriental thought. Mr. Leonard wasn't much interested in Oriental thought, of course, but he was oddly fascinated by certain thoughtful Westerners of his own imagination, who "stayed

home to hallucinate": sex was "the coin of this imaginative realm," according to Mr. Leonard, "a displacement of political power, of scavenging. While we gen-
eralized about race, mind, culture, and nation, we
masturbated."

Meanwhile, the Agonizing Reappraisals continued.
The unhappy "artist" who had once volunteered to
massage a portion of his raw material in a Soho gallery
gave voice to the growing fear: "I lecture and do short-
term teaching gigs and get an occasional grant," he said
bravely; "but the grant thing is wearing itself out. Many
of us have already had two National Endowment grants
and one Guggenheim and that's all there is." The grant-
ee had just received another five thousand bucks from
the Hirshhorn Museum in exchange for his latest exhibition (a huge aluminium merry-go-round), but he was
still unhappy: "Even the biggest grant, the Guggenheim, is hardly enough to pay for one of these installa-
tions. The only time I can work is when there's some
money to start something, like this show." The problem, it seemed, was that nobody would buy the stuff
anymore. As a fellow exhibitor at the same show put it:
"Who would want them, where would they put them.
You can't *give* them away. We've tried. I never thought
I'd be building things that I couldn't give away."

The curator at the Hirshhorn tried to summon up
some of the old spirit. "History may not conclude that
each of these artists is as important as Picasso," he said
plaintively, "but the mission upon which they have
embarked...is no less deliberate and courageous than

the revolutions of the French Cubists or the Russian Futurists.'' The words trailed off. It seemed that folks didn't really give a damn about the Picassos and the Cubists and the Futurists anymore: there were much scarier things on television. By the time the museum's aging futurists got around to sponsoring one more musical tribute to their favorite rock singer of the 1960s, there was an unmistakable odor of antiquity in the air. New had become old; In had become Out; shocking had become quaint. One more time.

As for the Artist himself, he was nostalgic, not only for the days when his neighbors in the artistic community had been interested in his onanistic visions, but for the days when the suckers had come to see him bite himself all over and pull out all his body hair. ''It was far cheaper when I was using my own body,'' he sighed. Oh well, ''if the idea of making studio art bothers me too much, I can always think of myself as a guerilla fighter making a bomb in his basement.''

Things were no better on the upper decks. Truman Capote did find time to publish a new batch of ''nonfiction short stories'' just before the ''envy'' set in, but it was not a happy occasion. ''I'm an alcoholic. I'm a drug addict. I'm homosexual. I'm a genius,'' announced Mr. Capote hopefully, only to be met by an awkward critical silence. It was quite a comedown from the days when Mr. Capote had been able to think of himself as—wait for it—''a planet wanderer.'' In those days, he had been ''a Sahara tourist approaching through darkness desert tents and desert campfires where dangerous natives lurk,'' and so forth. Trouble was, nobody seemed to care much about the Wanderer's problems anymore, which must have come as something of a shock over at *People* magazine, where the Capote literature was being published in 1980.

Predictably, the new stories were notable chiefly for the insights they afforded into the fifty-five-year-old genius's own philosophy of habitual self-abuse: "Whatever would we do without Mother Fist and her Five Daughters? They've certainly been a friendly bunch to us through the years," etc. One or two reviewers were excited by Mr. Capote's account of his discovery of an electric sexual device ("the shape of an average-sized" male member, according to its well-informed discoverer), but when the guys had finished debating the meaning of Mr. Capote's stimulatory machine, there just wasn't much else to talk about—only some carelessly-plotted murder stories, and, inevitably, some old Marilyn Monroe anecdotes that gave the author a chance to show off huge chunks of his latent genius: "Marilyn! Marilyn, why did everything have to turn out the way it did? Why does life have to be so f—king rotten?"

Mr. Capote may have been asking for it with that one, but nobody wanted to be too rude, so the question remained unanswered. By the same token, critical silence reigned as Mr. Capote recalled the day that he had first wished aloud to be a female, the day he had first understood that his whole life would be soured by the derision that would almost certainly attend such an ambition. The consensus was that it was really a bit late in Mr. Capote's game to explain to him that the derision he would continue to encounter for the remainder of his life would be directed not at his emotional problems—he was, like everybody else, what he was—but at his conviction that the perpetual public celebration of those problems constituted a sort of art, an acceptable substitute for actual literature or thought.

The novelist Mary Renault must have seen 1980 coming back in 1953. "They were specialists," she had written. "They had not merely accepted their limitations...bringing an extra humility to the hard study of human experience. They had identified themselves with their limitations, they were making a career of them. They had turned from all other reality, and curled up in them snugly, as in a womb."

Folks tried to be polite, of course, it was that kind of town. The neighbors from *Vogue* came over with a basket of leftover critical goodies and said that Mr. Capote's new book was, well, "taut," if you knew what they meant. Also "honest," of course, terribly terribly "honest," and that was a pretty good thing to be, wasn't it? Nobody objected to their little gesture, but both sides of the street were a little embarrassed when Mordecai Richler of the Book-of-the-Month Club said that the August Selection charted the "journey and obsessions" of an "important American writer"; and when Walter Clemons of *Newsweek* said that the horrid little volume was "the most enjoyable book I've read this year," he just sounded like...well, he sounded like someone imitating a *Newsweek* book critic. John Fowles took a flying leap at the non-existent bandwagon when he tried to persuade the readers of the *Saturday Review* that Mr. Capote was "as good as sheer literary intelligence can make a writer," but he hit the earth with a painful literary whimper: "Capote's deliciously convincing account of an afternoon with Marilyn Monroe is by several miles the best thing I have ever read on her," said Mr. Fowles, trying to pretend he'd said something worth saying. It just wasn't like old times at all.

True, the English teacher who took care of the book for the *Washington Post* said that it was all "simply stunning," my dears, and that Mr. Capote was, you know, "a major writer," who had produced another "marvelous piece of writing," and also some "brilliant renderings" that made for "superb reading," and all that sort of thing. "Trust these tales," he pleaded, but nobody would. As a matter of fact, the class had started nodding off after the bit about the "renderings" ("renderings," like "illuminations of the human condition" and "transactions of the human experience," are *always* a bad sign). Pretty soon the English teacher quieted down and shuffled off to Dartmouth, where, we're horrified to say, he taught classes in American literature.

All in all, it was a pretty flat Publishing Event, and only the most venerable among us could even remember a time when Truman Capote had been, in the words of Random House, "one of the master stylists of our time," and "a master of English prose," a time when Norman Mailer had been able to refer to the Master Stylist as "the most perfect writer of my generation."

And where *was* Norman Mailer, in this time of crisis? Well, "the most important literary figure of his generation" (Grove Press) was touring the television talk shows, trying to "vend" his latest "creation," and wondering what had happened to all his youthful dreams. "It's a poor way for a grown man to live," sighed the former literary figure: "perched on a stage full of pale orange and pale blue plastic furniture, hot lights up, your stomach rumbling." And when Mr. Mailer wasn't vending and rumbling in front of the cameras, he was writing long books about old movie stars and selling pieces of those books to the women's magazines. At one point the Important Vendor even called in a reporter from one of those magazines in order to announce that he was, believe it or not, "the 'ghost' of Marilyn Monroe." Sure enough, the ghost was trying to Vend its latest Creation: "I expect people to jump on this book and say 'How dare he!' " cried Mr. Mailer, somewhat wistfully. If there are any ghost-watchers out there who are still interested in jumping on Mr. Mailer, they should please give him a call. He is waiting, and it would be a kindness.

To draw attention to these individual cultural embarrassments—to these exposures, if you will—is also to describe the fundamental deficiency (and the fatal weakness) of an entire class of self-proclaimed artists and thinkers. The quivering guardians of the old order were pleasant, clever people, on the whole, but they were not especially interesting or cultivated people, and they were certainly not serious people. Most of them had fallen into what they thought of as the life of the mind much as they might once have fallen into a life of ballroom dancing, or real-estate speculation. Just as the younger sons of the colonial centuries had joined the cavalry or the church simply because one had to join something, so had many of the children of the first age of mass public education drifted into the service of popular "art" and "education" and cultural arbitration simply because they had nowhere else to go. They were artistic and philosophical xenophobes without intellectual definition or social purpose, even in their own minds—fuzzy minds devoid of soul, pretentious craftsmen devoid of discipline, the ubiquitous Babbitts of the second half of the twentieth century. As a class, they were the people that Arnold of Rugby had seen coming when he cautioned his future biographer Arthur Stanley against the cultivation of cleverness for its own sake: "Mere intellectual acuteness," said the Doctor, "divested as it is, in too many cases, of all that is comprehensive and great and good, is to me more revolting than the most helpless imbecility, seeming to be almost like the spirit of Mephistopheles."

The disciplined Doctor had been a villainous authoritarian, in Lytton Strachey's jealous eyes, but he would have seemed an alien monster to Strachey's intellectual descendants, had they been conversant with either Strachey or Arnold. The progeny of resentment had embraced their cultural isolation (and its attendant ignorance) as a matter of artistic principle; and because they knew so little of the purposes or the history of life, they knew even less of art. Inevitably, they had tried to divorce the art from the life—to make a closed shop of the human psychology and spirit—and in doing so they had signed their own cultural death warrants, the warrants that were finally being read aloud in the late 1970s and early 1980s. "Any teaching...which attempts to separate the poet from the man as though his excellence were to be measured by a radically different set of tests is, to my mind, either erroneous or trifling and superficial," said

Leslie Stephen, in his essay on Carlyle's ethics; this was "the fundamental doctrine of all sound criticism, whether of art or literature or life."

But if the cultural exiles knew Sir Leslie at all, they knew him as the father of Virginia Woolf (and Virginia Woolf, they recalled, had been mentioned in a play by Edward Albee, which had been made into a movie, which everybody had gone to see because it had been directed by Mike Nichols, who was a monument): "fundamental doctrines" had no place in the neighborhoods of professional uncertainty and institutionalized triviality. The cultural establishment had deliberately rendered itself "trifling and superficial" over a period of forty or fifty years, and by 1980 it had become a bloated irrelevance, a dead weight that the artistic conscience of the larger society was no longer willing to listen to or support. Like the younger sons in the outposts of empire in 1903, the cultural philistines of 1980 were suddenly in the way, an obstacle to artistic growth and intellectual advance, an embarrassment to the literary democracy that had spawned them, aging relics of a vanished order of civic immaturity. The philistines were never to know it, but their true enemies were progress, and civilization, and—most of all—time. With the legions of the past, the present, and the future arrayed against it, the postwar American cultural community looked, in a word, silly. Scared silly.

Chapter IV

The Golden Age

There was still plenty of brave talk, of course. Some of it surfaced when the *New York Times Book Review* distributed a little questionnaire around the community to find out if any of the residents still thought they were "really living, as one critic put it, in a Golden Age of the American Novel." Now, it goes without saying that people who are living in a Golden Age of anything do not spend their afternoons asking one another if they are really living in a Golden Age, but the stragglers of 1980 didn't know this, and the response to the questionnaire was almost touching in its fevered loyalty to the dead faith. Yes, yes, they *were* living in a Golden Age, said everybody tearfully, and it was going to get better and better, and everything was going to be All Right.

Typical in the insistence of his response was a clever

44

young writer of explicitly erotic novels named Scott Spencer. Mr. Spencer—a hard-working lad who had cornered the market in scenes of anal intercourse among teenagers, who had applied more gooey adjectives to certain rarely-seen adolescent muscles than any other specialist in the Community—this Mr. Spencer, we say, strongly suspected that "the future" would "deem" the novelists of his time "as among the ablest America has known." The earnest young clinician left it up to "future literary journalists" to decide exactly how his novelists would compare with "the great American novelists of the past"—"how William Styron compares with Thomas Wolfe," for instance, and, even more oddly, "how Philip Roth compares with Nathaniel Hawthorne"—but his own mind was already made up: the literature in question was "prospering" mightily, and the Age was Golden, yes it was it was it *was*.

The novelist Joyce Carol Oates couldn't have agreed more: "It is likely that we live in the very best of times," she sighed vaguely, and it was as close as she'd ever come to making a flat statement about anything. Alas, Ms. Oates was a professor of creative writing (at Princeton), and so it wasn't long before she found herself talking, as so often before, about "the imaginative freedom of the novelist in his or her craft," and about the "wild and surrealist employment" of "historical and nonfiction elements" in "the service of a metaphoric vision," and that kind of thing. Ms. Oates wasn't one to look for her metaphoric vision in the "didacticism of a Dos Passos," mind you (conservative metaphoric visions were always didactic): what she had in mind was something along the lines of the "sleight-of-hand of an E. L.

Doctorow" (liberal metaphoric visions were always accompanied by a little sleight of hand). The professor took a rather timid slap at the dread "19th century, when brainless moralizing romances sold in the millions," and then scurried back to the service of her metaphoric vision: "I anticipate lyricism and airiness, luxuriant space, the freedom to attempt virtually anything within the elastic confines of the novel," she hummed, sounding eerily like the William Styron of a happier age. "There is an exhilarating challenge in making prose outrageous and beautiful and idiosyncratic," said Ms. Oates, and her face wasn't even red.

The Let's Pretend We're Living In A Golden Age game was not a new one. For decades the entire cultural establishment had been putting itself to sleep at night by telling itself over and over again that it was a truly stupendous little cultural establishment, probably the most important little cultural establishment that had ever existed. It had been an age of cut-rate Homers and dime-a-dozen Dantes, of daily Cultural Events and weekly Artistic Epochs, an age bracketed by congratulatory self-delusion and defined by the proximity of its own horizons, an age when everything was Great precisely because nothing was very good. It had been the age of Capote and Warhol and Updike and Pollock masquerading as the age of Pericles, and even in its death throes it shamed itself and its parent countries with the shabbiness of its bravado.

It was the shabbiness of a self-induced cultural deprivation, the bravado of an entrenched provincialism: the game of Golden Age had been played for so long that nobody knew it was a game anymore. When the columnist Anthony Lewis said that a recent book about Ways of Lying was "exceptionally important," he didn't really mean that it was *important*: he meant that it was important within the context of the game, which was the only context that Anthony Lewis had ever known. He would have said the same for any stray work of the imagination, and frequently did. And so did everybody else, of course: it was a time when all things were important because nothing was. If Mr. Lewis could say that his book of the moment was "exceptionally" important, then there was nothing to stop his old colleague Harrison Salisbury from saying that a new book about animals was not only "important," but "myth-shattering" as well. If the *New York Times Book Review* could say that some new CIA memoirs were "important," if Professor Wolff of Brandeis could say that *The Age of Structuralism* was "an important contribution to contemporary intellectual history," if the London *Times* could rule that a new novel from Paul Theroux was "indisputably important," then why shouldn't Gaddis Smith tell the readers of *Foreign Affairs* that *The National Interest and the Human Interest* was "a book of major importance"? For that matter, why shouldn't the critic Jonathan Yardley go a step further and pretend that a new collection of Ernest Hemingway's semiliterate letters was "a book of enormous importance"? After all, Peter Prescott of *Newsweek* had already said that the volume had deepened his understanding of "one of America's most important writers."

A staff writer for *Ms.* magazine insisted that something called *Women of Crisis* was "one of the most important books on women to appear in the last decade," a blurb-writer at Doubleday was all wrapped up in "the most important book about women since *My Mother, My Self,*" and a volume of what an anonymous fan at the *Washington Star* thought of as "high-class pornography" was also, according to the same writer, by "one of the most important women writers of the twentieth century." But then, the dying *Star* was under a lot of pressure from the rival gang at the *Washington Post*, which had just announced that the latest recording by one rock singer was "a minor work from a major artist," and that the latest from another was "a major work by a major artist." An offering from still a third contestant (Bruce Springsteen) was also "a major work by a major artist," but it was apparently more major than other major works: "Pop records," said the standard-setters at the *Post*, "don't get much more important than that."

Under the circumstances, one had to be at least a little bit grateful to the crew at Delta Books, who left the door wide open by declaring that a new biography of Velikovsky was only "as important as Velikovsky's books themselves." One also had to feel a certain sympathy for one well-known novelist and English professor (since deceased), who finally threw in his inky towel and decided that everything he'd ever seen or heard was Immensely Important. William Styron's latest book was "immensely important." *Three Farms (Making Milk, Meat and Money from the American Soil)* was "immensely important." Even Joyce Carol Oates's novel of the week was "immensely important." The best-selling idolater didn't go so far as to admit that he himself was Immensely Important, but he lost no time in announcing the establishment of his own magazine, which would publish *only* "the famous writers and artists of the future." The professor wasn't going to be caught short again: he was going to make damn sure he had a reliable list of "the next generation of great writers, poets, and visual artists."

Of course, it was just barely possible that some of the books (if not the records) *were* genuinely important— after all, important books do get written, every once in a while (Marcus Aurelius wrote one, and so did Montaigne, and Goethe, and quite a few other people). And therein lay the tragedy of the awful spectacle: the few serious books of the grimly flippant century were being buried by the avalanche of mass-produced "importance." When Professor Riley of Wisconsin hailed one of these serious volumes (William Galston's *Justice and the Human Good*) as "a fine and important book," he may well have been speaking the simple truth; but what chance did the occasional honest "fine" have against the ritualistic chants of "stupendous" and "enormous" and "myth-shattering"? Those reviewers and authors who still spoke the simple truths were, like the young men and women who told the truth on job résumés, victims of the general hype of a democracy gone haywire, their words and accomplishments devalued by the automatic dishonesty of the competition. What passed for an intellectual community in 1980 was more than happy to sacrifice its few genuinely helpful writers on the altar of majesty for all; and the victims of the dark age could draw small comfort from the knowledge that the grandchildren of the Immensely Important generation would be chuckling at the memory of their ancestors, fifty years on, as they swept the enormous piles of profundity into the trash.

"Among the smaller duties of life," said the adorable Sydney Smith, "I hardly know any one more important than that of not praising where praise is not due. Reputation is one of the prizes for which men contend.... It produces more labor and more talent than twice the wealth of a country could ever rear up. It is the coin of genius, and it is the imperious duty of every man to bestow it with the most scrupulous justice and the wisest economy."

Chapter V

Being the Best

Reputations born of hyperbole must gather ever more hyperbolic hyperbole unto themselves, else they die (and take their fabricators with them). The problem, of course, is that there is a point above which a reputation cannot rise: once a writer has become the most important writer of the day, he or she has nowhere to go but down, or back to work. That was one of the messy problems facing the cultural authorities in the time of the great panic. Not only had the highest wave finally been sighted and engaged, but everybody seemed to be reaching the top of the wave at almost the same moment. A thousand middle-aged professors of creative writing had suddenly become Immensely Important rivals of Shakespeare, and the decks rang with cries of praise as the passengers fought over the last little tittle of hyperbole, the critical adjective that might lift its recipient—and, not so incidentally, its donor—an inch above the teeming professorial masses, if only for a heady moment or two.

Joyce Carol Oates, for instance, had written so many Immensely Important stories and novels that she had long since become, in John Gardner's somewhat flustered view, "one of the great writers of our time." Which wasn't saying much, in the era of universal and mandatory majesty. After all, P. D. James had only been writing mysteries for a few years, and the *Wall Street Journal* had already lifted her "to the ranks of the best novelists," right up there with the likes of Walker Percy ("the best novelist we now have," according to Jonathan Yardley of the *Washington Star*), William Burroughs ("our one genius," in the eyes of Norman Mailer), and John Updike ("America's finest novelist" at the *Washington Post*, "second to none in our time" at the *Hudson Review*). It was a time of desperate superlative, a time when John Leonard could say that the columnist Murray Kempton "writes better than anyone else," a time when Robert Penn Warren—himself "America's finest living poet," according to Random House—could say that Katherine Anne Porter had been "unsurpassed in our century or country—perhaps any time or country—as a writer of fiction in the short forms," only to be out-classed by Walter Clemons of *Newsweek*: "Elizabeth Bowen is simply one of the best story writers who ever lived."

This last was a variation on the Quite Simply Bluff, which was used to disarm the enemy whenever one was about to make a particularly sweeping award, as in "Quite simply, *Dispatches* is the best book to have been written about the Vietnam War" (*New York Times Book Review*), or "John Hawkes and Kurt Vonnegut are simply the most original first-rate writers in this country" (this from John Irving, who had—quite simply—freaked out on the "erotic power" of Mr. Hawkes' language). It showed up in the *National Review*, of all places, ("Henry Hazlitt is, quite simply, the best writer on economic subjects we have going, and has been that for better than four decades") and Doris Grumbach used it to turn a sleazy novel of "troubled chaos, pornographic excess and psychic violence" into one more Grumbachian pussycat: "Quite simply, it is the most imaginative, solid and satisfying novel of this year, or of the year past." And it finally found its way into the *New York Review*'s subscription campaigns: "Quite simply, you don't pay a cent."

The Quite Simply Bluff was excessively precious Critic Talk for Let's Have a Moment Of Awed Silence Here, and it was offensive because it was purposely used in exactly those contexts where it should not have been used, where the issue was not Simple at all but rather the opposite. Sir Henry Savile (one of the scholars who prepared the King James Version of the Bible) read the indictment, almost four centuries ago: "Vanity," he said, "is the sin, and affectation is the punishment: the first may be called the root of self-love, the other the fruit. Vanity is never at its full growth till it spreadeth into affectation, and then it is complete."

Because all affectation is, as Carlyle observed more than once, based on falsehood, it always tends—like falsehood itself—to absurdity. Just as a social climber makes a fool of himself by denying his origins and

making loud remarks about rich people he has known
and loved, so did the literary butterflies expose themselves to ridicule by abandoning "good writers" and
"bad writers" in favor of "Finest Living Writers" and
"Distinguished Living Authors" and "Important
Voices In Fiction" and "Major Prose Stylists." A good
writer named Nicholas Delbanco, for instance, was
"purely and simply, splendid," according to the novelist George Garrett, but Mr. Delbanco was also "as fine
a pure prose stylist as any writer living," if one could
believe the *Chicago Tribune*, and of course one wanted
to. V.S. Pritchett—"the finest English writer alive," in
the eyes of the critic Frank Kermode—might have been
content to think of William Trevor as "one of the finest
short story writers at present writing in the Anglo-Irish
mode," whatever that meant, but he nursed a growing
suspicion that the late Henry Green had been "the most
gifted prose writer of his generation." Bad luck for
Tony Powell, who was merely "one of the finest novelists in the English language in the twentieth century," according to his diffident American publishers.
Doris Grumbach thought that John Updike was
"probably the most supple prose stylist we have" (an
appropriate variation, given the peculiar nature of Mr.
Updike's literary interests); Robert Towers had the odd
idea that Randall Jarrell had written "the funniest
prose ever written by an American poet"; Charles Lar-
son of the *Detroit News* had it on good authority that
James Baldwin was "one of the major prose stylists of
the last thirty years"; and Simon and Schuster were
determined to persuade the world that their man Graham Greene was "the most distinguished living writer

in the English language," even as their man was taking a reporter from *Newsweek* aside to reveal that "Borges and Garcia-Marquez and some of the other Latin American writers" were "the best there are today."

The artists themselves—and some of the people we have just mentioned were genuine artists—were victims as well as victors. Mr. Greene, for example, had acquired his own title entirely by accident. It had happened on a perfectly ordinary day in that hot summer of 1980. The seventy-six-year-old Prose Stylist had been minding his own business, puttering about in the back yard, perhaps, when all of a sudden he slipped and fell into a nest of hungry Anglo-American literati. It was all over in a matter of minutes: Mr. Greene had become— Quite Simply—the Most Distinguished Living Whatever, and there wasn't a damn thing he could do about it.

He should have seen it coming, of course. As long ago as 1948, Jean Stafford had said that Mr. Greene's latest novel was "the best book I have read by a living writer in years." At about the same time, the old *New York Herald Tribune Book Review* had said that the novelist ranked with "the most talented users of the English language today." If Mr. Greene had been more attentive, he might have heard the drums beginning to roll. Quietly, at first: "One of the ablest writers of our time" (J.B. Priestley); "One of the really significant novelists now writing in any language" (Sean O'Faolain). And then more insistently: "Among the few, the very few, of our great living novelists" (Elizabeth "Best Story Writer" Bowen, 1961); "In my view, the outstanding living British author" (Philip French, *Financial Times*, 1969).

Simon and Schuster got their toes wet in 1971—"the most distinguished living novelist in the English language"—and dived in in 1972: "The greatest living novelist in the English language." But this was too much, and all the other greatest living prose stylists were offended by Mr. Greene's end run. There were feeble efforts at retrenchment ("one of the most prodigious and effective English novelists," *Washington Post*, 1973; "the most accomplished of English novelists," *New York Times*, 1978; "on his good days, [he] probably *is* the greatest living English novelist, in both the stylistic and the intellectual senses, if not in the spiritual sense," Bryan Griffin, 1979), and eventually even Simon and Schuster retreated to the relative obscurity of "the greatest of living *English* novelists" (emphasis ours). Still, the outcome was never really in doubt, and at the time of the great crash of 1980, Mr. Greene was, like everybody else, Quite Simply the Most Distinguished.

Predictably but unfortunately, this particular Most Distinguished had prepared for the crash by producing "the best espionage novel ever written" (UPI), which created the most Godawful confusion, since the Most Distinguished had himself said that a book by John Le Carré was "the best spy story I have ever read." ("It may be the best anybody has ever read," huffed Orville Prescott at the time, trying to keep up but breathing hard.) Even Lord Snow had said that Mr. Le Carré was "the best writer of spy stories, living or dead," which was bad news for Maugham and Ambler and Fleming and Buchan and all the rest of the also-rans. Still, had Lord Snow lived, surely he would have been forced to go with the flow, and to concede with *Bookviews* magazine that Mr. Greene was *"the* master of the spy novel." In those days, rules were rules.

And what of Mr. Greene himself? "He did not comment on his ascension, in his seventy-sixth year, to the position of pre-eminence among British writers," complained Walter Clemons of *Newsweek*. And it was no wonder. After all, what's a fellow to do? Who *was* the best, anyway, damn it?

And the answer came back: We all are.

Chapter VI

The Historical Fantasy

It is indeed strange how prepossessions and delusions seize upon whole communities of men; no basis in the notion they have formed, yet everybody adopting it, everybody finding the whole world agree with him in it, and accept it as an axiom of Euclid.... This people cannot be convinced out of its "axiom of Euclid" by any reasoning whatsoever; on the contrary, all the world assenting, and continually repeating and reverberating, there soon comes that singular phenomenon, which the Germans call *Schwärmerey* ...which means simply "Swarmery," or the "Gathering of Men in Swarms," and what prodigies they are in the habit of doing and believing, when thrown into that miraculous condition.

Thomas Carlyle

The fundamental fantasy of the century's "artistic community"—that it was, in fact, an artistic community—

was born largely of historical ignorance. Just as their isolation from normal human experience and aspiration made it almost impossible for the Major Artists to understand why so many healthy citizens seemed to view the Community as an increasingly bizarre and irrelevant oddity, so did their historical isolation blind them to the absurdity of their pretensions. The boys and girls could not pull up their socks and do better, because they did not know what better was: they really believed that they were the best of their time, and many of them believed that they were the best of all time.

So it was that when the rock critic who doubled as "literary editor" for *Rolling Stone* magazine said that a long novel by John Irving had "a strange, *Moby-Dick*-like sense of completeness," nobody laughed or even blushed, because nobody saw the joke. After all, the lad was just doing his bit for the defense of the realm, saying exactly the sort of thing that everybody had been taught to say; he knew that any long novel had to bear a resemblance to either Melville or Proust, because that's what those dudes *wrote*, you know—long novels, Just Like Mr. Irving. The representative from *Rolling Stone* was just the newest member of a community that traced its understanding of art and life to vague memories of grand titles on a tenth-grade reading list, and elevated that understanding to a principle of criticism and finally of survival.

It was this principle that prompted John Irving to say of an interminable erotic saga by John Casey that it "closely resembles *Remembrance of Things Past*"; that required the poet James Dickey to say of an old war novel by Thomas Boyd that there was "no battle scene in Tolstoy's *War and Peace* to equal the drama and terror of Boyd's account''; that encouraged Leonard Michaels to say in the *New York Times Book Review* that a dreary scatological farce from Joseph Heller "combined Einstein's theory of relativity with Kafka's agonies''; that permitted a staff writer for the *Saturday Review* to say of a memoir by Oriana Fallaci that it was "a work of transcendent Greek tragedy''; that permitted Seymour Krim to say in the *Washington Post* that William Burroughs smacked of "Theodore Dreiser at his most powerful''; that permitted the novelist Paul Theroux to say of a new travel book that it was "as wise as *Walden*,'' and that encouraged a critic from *Newsday* to say that a new adventure from Philip Caputo was reminiscent of "the best of Joseph Conrad.'' Before it was all over, even the columnist Ellen Goodman found herself saying that "Picasso dominates art the way Shakespeare dominates literature or Mozart dominates music,'' confirming widespread suspicions that even the smartest members of the class (and Ms. Goodman was pretty smart) knew almost as much about art as they did about music. "The worst of this artist is very, very good,'' sighed Ms. Goodman, in her own variation on the Quite Simply Bluff.

Ms. Goodman's remarks were interesting precisely because they did come from a writer of her intelligence. As Waugh put it:

> The large number of otherwise cultured and intelligent people who fall victims to Señor Picasso are not posers. They are genuinely "sent." It may seem preposterous to those of us who are immune, but the process is apparently harmless. They

emerge from their ecstasy as cultured and intelligent as ever. We may even envy them their experience. But do not let us confuse it with the sober and elevating happiness which we derive from the great masters.

The Picasso Factor

Let us pause for a moment and consider, with our customary objectivity, the Picasso "ecstasy." If we can begin to explain that phenomenon, we may be on our way to understanding the fundamental character of the larger historical and social oddity that was the massive "cultural community" of the second half of the twentieth century.

The first thing we must do is get the stale smoke out of our eyes. Which is to say that we must start afresh, and concede publicly what most earnest men and women have always conceded privately, that the ancient apology for bad art—"the work is shoddy and disjointed because The Times are shoddy and disjointed"—is pretty much nonsense. We say "pretty much" because, like lesser axioms of the creative-writing classes ("the artist must be original," "the art must be concrete," "art mirrors life," "art must be upsetting," etc.), the apology for bad art has just a shading of minor truth to it, just enough validity to render it attractive to bad artists and worse critics. The slogan appeals, in other words, to the ego of the third-rate; and—like the lesser axioms of the creative-writing class—it was never meant to be taken seriously by the first-rate, or even the second. It was primarily a hastily invented rationalization, a temporary excuse whipped up in the final decades of the nineteenth century to justify something that already existed. The "something," of course, was bad art; but—and this is the crucial point—it was bad art that was also *popular* art, in certain severely defined neighborhoods.

The increasing popularity of bad art in the early years of the twentieth century was, like the art itself, one of the inevitable legacies of the first decades of genuine social and economic (and therefore cultural) democracy. The bad art was not a reflection or an elucidation of "bad times"; on the contrary, the art had been getting worse precisely because "the times," for the great mass of men, had been getting better. The art (and the art-criticism) had been getting worse because the democracy had been growing purer, and for no other reason. Beauty had become a business.

The explanation was simple enough: the true arbiters were gone. Whatever their economic and moral flaws, the old class divisions did ensure the existence, from generation to generation, of a genuine cultural "elite," of a small but fairly stable number of wealthy, well-educated citizens who could and did honor and preserve the cultural heritage of the West in their schools, their homes, their galleries and their souls. Accordingly, the gradual disintegration of the old class systems in the years before the second world war paved the way for the more general artistic and cultural collapse of the postwar years. When Waugh said (through one of his characters in *Brideshead Revisited*) that "all modern art" was "bosh," he was of course essentially correct (the word "bosh," after all, can be traced to a

Turkish word meaning "empty"); but even in 1945 it was not the sort of thing one could say in public. The judgement was *aesthetically* correct, but politically offensive: it was undemocratic. It was "elitist." Art had become politics, in many minds; and a criticism of "modern art" was, ipso facto, a criticism of the egalitarian principle. Criticize what the people created, and you criticized the people. Duncan Williams described the situation in his book, *Trousered Apes*:

> The compulsive hunt for equality can...be seen in the hatred of form and style which characterizes contemporary poetry, art and music. Nietzsche observed that strong natures enjoy their "finest gaiety" in the constraint of style, while, conversely, it is weak characters "without power over themselves" who hate such constraint. The traditional poet, artist and musician trained long and arduously for his vocation.... Since all cannot indulge in such intensive preparation, art must come down from its pedestal and make itself available to the masses. The result is poetry without the bothersome restraint of form, [art] in which anyone can indulge, and music which is so unprofessional by former standards that an amateur can quickly reproduce a passable rendering.

Pablo Picasso was not an artist in any legitimate sense of the word. As a young man, he had some technical skill (which he later mislaid), but very little aesthetic imagination or spiritual comprehension; and his oppressively primitive and imitative efforts never sparked any real interest among his more dedicated contemporaries, or among patrons of genuine art (which was beginning to be in short supply). Indeed,

Señor Picasso himself seems to have realized and accepted his limitations of character and talent at a fairly early age. He did his best for a few years at the beginning of his long career—until about 1905—but he quickly realized that his best was not good enough. His honest pictures were definitely pleasant (and there is nothing wrong with pleasant art), but they lacked what we may call "purpose," and they were indistinguishable from the equally pleasant work of fifty other young Picassos of the time. In other words, the kid wasn't going anywhere special, and he knew it.

But it was 1905, and the political and cultural democracy that was part of the legacy of the Victorian reform movements was beginning to extend its enticing tributaries into previously inviolate quarters. Young Picasso smelt the economic wave of the new century, and he threw his somewhat pudgy body into it. Wyndham Lewis told the story:

> With the coming of the welfare state, the virtual disappearance of the picture-buying rich-man, the collector of new pictures, the artist no longer has the temptation to grow rich. At the start of his career, he knows that what he paints has, as it were, no commercial value. There are various semi-charitable institutions, and now there are institutes, from which he can derive support if he pleases or impresses by his extremism. But there is nothing to be gained by painting a pleasant, a recognizable or comprehensible picture....

Señor Picasso's carefully calculated leap was a leap into self-conscious artistic extremism. It was a procedure that was to be repeated many times in the dreary decades to come: a young "artist" of average or less-than-average talent works hard for several years, painting or writing or sculpting or composing, and attracting no attention; and then he discovers that he *can* attract attention (and money) by making a spectacle of himself, or his work (it doesn't matter which)—and so he does. It was to be the route of Hemingway and Schönberg, of Jacob Epstein and Jackson Pollock, of Gertrude Stein and Henry Miller and all the idle graduates of all the creative-writing institutes in a bored and badly educated society. By 1980 the sea lanes were clogged with painted soup cans and Nonfiction Novels, with Theatres of the Absurd and muddy streams of consciousness, with "Erotic Epics" and "experimental prose" and horrid chunks of leftover cubism, with yesterday's avant-garde and tomorrow's Literary Events, with dead and dying Moderns and Post Moderns and Reductionists and Body Artists and Expressionists and Post Expressionists and Progressives and Beats and Ops and Pops, with all the sorry debris of a civilization lost at sea.

Picasso-art itself was often described by unkind but knowledgeable dealers and collectors as "wallpaper art" or "motel room art." Whence, then, the considerable notoriety of its creator, even in aggressively sophisticated circles? Ah, but the notoriety was its own source, and the whole point: Picasso-art might have been "bosh," as Waugh said, but it was *saleable* bosh. The Picasso-industry was an industry created by art dealers and art critics, but it was an industry aimed *at* the masses, and in particular at the mass of the Upwardly Mobile and superficially educated middle class, the nervous urbanites who liked to feel knowledgeable about art without having to know anything about life. Señor Picasso was the perfect vehicle for the initial assault on the new market: just passable enough to attract the necessary squeals from the anxious professional critics, just reputable enough to be discussed with a straight face, just inscrutable enough to support the con.

It was in part a social arrangement—a way of keeping the artistic plebes happy and out of the way—but it was primarily an economic and intellectual arrangement. The Picasso name was quite deliberately developed over the years as a money-making commodity, as a way of ensuring a fairly constant supply of funds and popular respectability for an entire community of idle hangers-on. Pablo Picasso (like his aesthetic progeny) gave the art students something to imitate, and he made the popular critics of the middle brow feel that they were really in-the-know, and very close to the cutting edge. He was thrown as a sop to the hip-shaking curators of "museums of modern art" and the would-be connoisseurs and the bored old party-goers and the ambitious young critics and the more gullible buyers— to the sort of people who now get their ideas about life and art from *Artforum* and *Newsweek*—and all the time the real art world continued to function much as it had always functioned, and dealers and collectors allowed themselves a smirk or two as they used the proceeds from Picassos to purchase good prints and copies of Titians and Turners and Tintorettos.

The artist Francis Bacon said it all (possibly inadvertently) when he said that painting had become "a game by which man distracts himself." "You may say that it has always been like that," said Mr. Bacon, "but now it's entirely a game. What is fascinating is that it's getting more difficult for the artist. He must really deepen the game to be any good at all, so he can make life a bit more exciting."

What happened to upset the balance was that a new generation came along, a generation that didn't realize that its Daddies and Mommies had been playing a game. Because the members of this new generation were unusually empty sorts, in the spiritual sense, they lacked the confidence to laugh at their parents' absurdities; they tried to adapt their own thinking to the atrocities they had read about and seen on the walls of their galleries, and many of the weaker ones succeeded in this effort. To many of them, the Picasso farce, and all it implied, was no longer a farce at all: it was art.

The spectacle of 1980, then, was the spectacle of a community that could no longer "emerge from the ecstasy": just as the adolescent who has memorized all the imposing titles on his reading list gradually comes to believe that he has actually read the books and absorbed their message, so had the twentieth-century Homers finally come to believe in their own cultural fantasies.

There was pity in it, but there was also humor. When the old pornographer Henry Miller finally went away, the *Washington Star* said a tearful little farewell to a "literary artist" and "a cultural monument," and said something pre-recorded about "an extraordinarily fresh and vigorous celebration of the passing show and the delights of embracing life without bourgeois bookkeep-

ing." What was revealing was not that certain editorial
writers for Major Newspapers enjoyed pornography,
and were willing to say so (it had been a long time since
anyone had accused American journalists of civility),
but that they no longer knew that it was turned out by
pornographers: they thought it was produced by "cultural monuments." In a horrible way, of course, it was.
By the same token, the novelist Michael Mewshaw
didn't think that Gore Vidal was a witty essayist or an
occasionally interesting novelist: he thought that Gore
Vidal was "a cultural commentator of profound importance." And so it went. The residents of the community
sensed that the waters were rising all about them, and
that they had lost control of the situation, but they did
not know what to do about it. So they held hands and
repeated the ancient tribal chants in ever more frenzied
tones: they passed out soiled invitations to Literary
Events, they offered still more Major Works, they promised beautiful Publishing Experiences, and always they
spoke of the importance of their bizarre Culture.

Joseph Heller produced a coarse comedy of absent
manners, and Jack Beatty of the *New Republic* said that
it was "a cultural event." Being Jack Beatty, he was
certainly only half serious, but other authorities were in
deadly earnest: *Publishers Weekly* had already asked
that *every* "new Heller novel" be declared "an event,"
and the motion was passed in tearful acclamation. Even
the innocent were used as cannon fodder: a perfectly
lucid book by David Storey, for instance, was transformed by his publishers into "an epic literary experience," and by the time the Experience reached the
Boston Globe the poor thing was "throbbing." The

Chicago Tribune Book World held the sad object at arm's length and concluded that "no one should be unmoved by this novel," before throwing it back into the ocean with the rest of that afternoon's epic literary experiences. In those final days, even the books that were not Epics or Experiences or Events throbbed so much that they became More Than Books, as in *"Sophie's Choice* is more than a novel, it is an act of conscience" *(John Barkham Reviews).* All the world had become one giant throbbing cultural binge.

Perhaps the lowest of many low points came when a "blue-ribbon commission" charged with supplying the White House with "great recordings reflecting the wide range of American cultural interests" decided to fulfill their 1980 responsibilities by awarding the President of their nation a copy of a new recording called *Never Mind the Bullocks,* by those great reflectors of the wide range of American cultural interests, the Sex Pistols. But the laugh was on the beribboned authorities, because the Sex Pistols weren't really monuments to the American culture at all; they were monuments to the culture of the United Kingdom. As if to apologize for their mistake, the members of the President's panel threw in copies of such Anglo-American classics as *Hard Core Jollies,Trout Mask Replica, Bad Girls, Hot Rats,* and—somewhat revealingly—*Crisis? What Crisis?*

Thomas Carlyle was fond of having the last word; and what he said of the social order in the nineteenth century he might also have said of the cultural fantasies of the twentieth:

> If a thing have grown so rotten that it yawns palpable, and is so inexpressibly ugly that the eyes

of the very populace discern it and detest it,—bring out a new pot of varnish with the requisite supply of putty; and lay it on handsomely. Don't spare varnish; how well it will all look in a few days, if laid on well! Varnish alone is cheap and is safe; avoid carpentering, chiselling, sawing and hammering on the old quiet House;—dry-rot is in it, who knows how deep; don't disturb the old beams and junctures: varnish, varnish, if you will be blessed by gods and men! Mendacity hanging in the very air we breathe; all men become, unconsciously or half or wholly consciously, *liars* to their own souls and to other men's; grimacing, finessing, periphrasing, in continual hypocrisy of *word*, by way of varnish to continual past, present, future misperformance of *thing*.... From a Population of that sunk kind, ardent only in pursuits that are low and in industries that are sensuous and *beaverish*, there is little peril of *human* enthusiasm....

Chapter VII

The Language of Criticism

The primary function of the professional critic in those dark days was to camouflage the true state of cultural affairs by obscuring the hollow center of the community with a smokescreen of pretentious prose. As we have seen, a special code had been developed over the years to make the job easier. In the language of the code, writers were "major prose stylists" or "magicians," stories were "fictions," ideas were "perceptions" ("perceptions of power," more often than not), squalor was "reality," goodness was "sentimentality," and life itself was just a bowl of the Multitudinous Transactions of The Human Condition (which were usually by John Updike). The tactic itself was very old—talk long enough and loud enough and confidently enough, and maybe the congregation won't notice that you aren't saying anything—but the weapons were the weapons of the first age of widespread idleness and mass literacy: typewriters and word processors and boredom and jargon and—most of all—fear. Fear of silence.

There was a strong element of unenlightened self-interest behind the never-ending chatter. When Peter Prescott of *Newsweek* (who was, in fact, one of the more honest reviewers of his day) said that Joyce Carol Oates's "fictions" were "seductive" because they had a "sense of the irrational in them," he wasn't just enjoying an unusually silly morning, he was making a very deliberate little bow to the Profundity God, and he wanted very much to be noticed in the act: a story, after all, was just a story, but a "fiction" fairly reeked of importance—ergo, people who were "seduced" by "fictions" were ever so much more important than book reviewers who just liked irrational stories.

By the same token, when William Golding wrote a good novel (and it was a good novel), Doris Grumbach was afraid to say that "William Golding has written a good novel." She had to get down on her literary hands and knees and make her daily obeisance to the fat little idol of professional criticism: "You may be quite sure that English novelist William Golding will be remembered in the history of literature as an inventive and original maker of fictions." In less important centuries, this would have been known as "using twenty-six words to do the work of seven," but in the twentieth century it was called "style." Ms. Grumbach had "much admired" Mr. Golding's previous book "for its portraits of modern monsters, a physically maimed boy born in the fires of the London blitz and other young moral freaks," but she was even more ecstatic about the new Fiction, because it had left her "with a sense of the mystery of existence integral to its formlessness," by which she meant to say that it was a really high-class type of book but she'd run out of space so could she stop now please.

The connoisseur of portraits of "young moral freaks" couldn't stop for long, though, because the third-class passengers were gaining on her: when Robert Coover's dirty stories had first appeared in skin magazines like *Cavalier* and *Playboy* and *Olympia*, they were just dirty stories, but by the time E.P. Dutton had shoved them between reasonably hard covers they had become "fictions" that "challenge the assumptions of our age," which was E.P. Dutton talk for God This Is Hot Stuff We Promise. Why hell, Mr. Coover's fictions used "the fabulous to probe beyond randomly perceived events," they were "weapons that counterpoint our consciousness, that show us the need for new modes of perception." Which *must* have been what Joyce Carol Oates was trying to say when she said (in the *Southern Review*, of all places), that Mr. Coover existed "blatantly and brilliantly in his fiction as an authorial consciousness." Or, perhaps not. In any case, the Coover fictions were "not human," they were "magic" (also Hot Stuff).

Ms. Oates had to say all those funny things because E.P. Dutton had ruled that Mr. Coover's fictions were "beyond randomly perceived events," and Ms. Oates knew that "beyond" was a code word for profundity, as in *Beyond Anxiety, Beyond Biofeedback, Beyond Intellectual Sexism,* etc. "Beyond" didn't mean anything, but it sounded ever so important, and accordingly it had become a bit of a last resort, in the dark days of 1980.

Many of the kids had been *Beyond Freedom and Dignity* for years, of course, but now they were going *Beyond Reason, Beyond Monogamy, Beyond Within,* and—inevitably—*Beyond Jogging.* Some hell-raiser from *Time* magazine had even found some old Beatle recordings that "leaked suggestive bits of near-meaning that made beyond-sense." Now you know what *that* was all about.

Informing

But then, Beyond-Art, like Beyond-Thought, was almost always "suggestive." It was not actually composed, or written, or painted, nor was it about anything or characterized by any quality; it was merely Suggested, or Felt, or—most often—Informed.

The novelist Jay Neugeboren was giving somewhat excessive voice to this principle when he told the readers of the *Nation* that he liked stories that were "seen clearly and sharply and that had a voice informing them which was steady, severe, spare," stories in which "there was the sense of a particular life lived, one in which the history of that life, past and future, was suggested and felt beyond the beginning and end of the story." Mr. Neugeboren would have gone ape over Harry Crews, who claimed that all of *his* stories were "of necessity still informed by my notions of the world and of what it is to be caught in it." Mr. Crews meant that he had trouble writing about things he didn't know about, but—"of necessity"—he didn't dare come right out in front of everybody and admit it. It was ever so much safer to be Informed. It was this spirit that prompted a professor named George Hunt to insist that John Updike's sweaty tales of cunnilingus in the lunatic fringes of suburbia were "informed" by "Nature," and it was this spirit that allowed Joyce Carol Oates to say of another atrocity by the same author that it was "informed" by a delightfully "passionate and despairing cynicism."

In the same mood, Jack Kroll of *Newsweek* found himself applauding the director of a new production of *Hamlet* who hadn't "been afraid" to "lay hands on the sacred text": Of Necessity the deed had been done with "a passionate intelligence that informs the entire production." The director had informed the first scene of *Hamlet* by doing away with it, and he had informed the ghost of Hamlet's father by cutting the ghost of Hamlet's father out of the play. This was "a daring innovation." "Hamlet's dead father appears not as a specter but as a kind of Danish dybbuk muscling his way out of Hamlet's very bowels," explained Mr. Kroll: "Hamlet becomes a giant, unwilling ventriloquist's dummy as his father's voice is wrenched from his mouth in hair-raising sepulchral tones while [Hamlet's] body lashes, heaves and snaps in a fit of ectoplasmic epilepsy." Now *that* was Informed Beyond-Art.

Mr. Kroll seemed to be in a bit of an ectoplasmic tizzy himself, especially when he got to the bit about Hamlet "attacking Ophelia like a rapist in a New York alley." And the big fight scene was so *gross*, so *cool*: I mean it was "really vicious," and one rare treat for the Jack Krolls of the world, in a day when "movies have made most violence onstage look like charades." (Mr. Kroll was, of course, an inveterate moviegoer, and he was not afraid to apply his inimitable literary style to adventures he had seen on the silver screen: "*Body Heat* is hot stuff. Its steamy, sultry, sexy story comes off the screen in waves of imagery that sear your eyeballs.") As for Hamlet himself, well, it was inevitable: "Once in a generation an actor becomes by acclamation Hamlet-champion of the world," and Mr. Kroll and his fellow fight fans hadn't acclaimed a Hamlet-champion in, oh, three years or so. The new champion was "the most exciting actor since"—well, "since the young Marlon Brando," according to Mike Nichols (who—lest we forget—had begun his own cultural career as a night-club comedian).

All in all, the new production was "a paranoid's paradise," and the whole thing was full of "cosmic jitters and colliding antitheses," because the Hamlet-champion was "a paragon and a mess, the best and the brightest, whose fuses keep blowing," and so forth. Mr. Kroll never got around to saying just *why* it was a good production, but then one so rarely does, with Informed Beyond-Art. And anyway, the critic had to leave room for maneuver: the "purists" were out there, he said, and they might not share his ectoplasmic excitement; after all, the Paranoid's Paradise was fizzing with the "high voltage" of—you guessed it—"reality." Mr. Kroll was eager to squeeze his pet reality down the nation's throat before the purists made him look like a fool: "This most pertinently impertinent of modern 'Hamlets' should be seen in America," he roared, but somehow it sounded a bit weak, like the wheeze of a man who was swimming against the tide.

But if Mr. Kroll and his friends were already out of their depth in Shakespearean waters, plenty of other folks were still splashing about happily in shallower ponds, heedless of the approaching storm. The novelist Michael Mewshaw, for instance, couldn't stop Informing the works of Gore Vidal, even though he must have known that it was time for both of them to get inside. "Given the general view that Vidal is a man of questionable morals," said Mr. Mewshaw, "it is ironic that his most serious failing as a novelist is his determination to infuse his fiction with the same ethical concerns, the polemical intensity and the didactic spirit that inform his nonfiction." Which might well have been the case, but it didn't make the assemblage look any less wet.

Swarming

One of the soggiest of the literary refugees was the ubiquitous Doris Grumbach, who was trying to dry off her intellectual reputation with one of D.M. Thomas's Erotic Epics. "If this were not a review, and if the reader did not expect from it some descriptive analysis and summary, I would simply advise him to 'experience' the book," said Ms. Grumbach, in a somewhat snappish burst of candor. Ms. Grumbach was a former Artistic Information Officer who had transferred her loyalties to the new Department of Instruction: Mr. Thomas's Epic constituted an "affecting and influencing network that puzzles the reader, then intrigues him and finally instructs him in the complexities of the hidden life of the psyche, even if he has never read Freud."

Paul Gray of *Time*, on the other hand, was reminded by the same book that "fiction can amaze as well as inform." "It promises sex, violence, a woman stripped of her privacy, the sadistic pornography of totalitarianism," chortled Mr. Gray, who quickly put on a straight face and tried to sound grown up about the whole thing: "Such subjects should not be denied to serious writers," he said solemnly, which meant that Paul Gray could go ahead and read the sadistic porn because it was Serious sadistic porn. Even so, promised the Amazed But Serious reviewer, those who came to the novel "with prurient interests alone" would "quickly grow baffled and bored." Some elitists couldn't help noticing the revelatory "alone" in that sentence, but it was thought best to ignore the implications.

Which was easier resolved than done, as Mr. Gray began to ramble on about a thirteen-page "dream fugue of eroticism" and about a long sequence wherein everybody "made love incessantly and"—he said it before anybody could stop him—"imaginatively" (and *seriously* too, of course, always very seriously). "The woman's breasts flow with milk, which she gives freely to everyone," sang Mr. Gray, who had apparently misplaced his notes. He was rummaging through a particularly absurd novel, and he probably knew it, really, because he kept pulling himself up short in order to make stern remarks about the wonderful way in which the book managed to "transcend titillation," though he was very careful not to say just who had been so extraordinarily titillated in the first place. And then before you knew it the dear fellow would be back at the book, quoting with relish the bit in which the heroine wondered if she had, just possibly, "grown obsessed with sex," and giving special attention to the character's most profoundly precious remarks: "And if I'm not thinking about sex, I'm thinking about death." "Their milk flows," cooed Mr. Gray, who concluded his transcendental meditations with some hurried words about "fusing the dreams of self with the nightmare of history."

In those days, no review of a novel in which Dr. Freud was a character could be admitted to the circus if it did not contain the obligatory words about the Horrors of History (and very few critics bothered to review novels in which Dr. Freud was *not* a character). The words were a sort of magic incantation, and they were used to turn dozens of prissy little "erotic epics" into Informed Beyond-Art. It was this operation that Doris Grumbach was endeavoring to perform when she said that the book in question moved from "the sick soul of one woman to the cosmic horror of man's holocaustic violence against man." She meant that Mr. Thomas had killed off his sexy heroine in a Nazi concentration camp, after predictable adventures of the flesh which Mr. Gray would have been uniquely well-qualified to describe. Ms. Grumbach summed up all the fun with her increasingly tiresome trademark: "What a splendid book!"

But the waters had grown higher and wilder, and it had become difficult to distinguish Ms. Grumbach's cries from those of the terrified competition. "I have not been so thoroughly enveloped by a book since reading *Garp*," cried Laurie Stone of the *Village Voice*, trying to jump from one envelope to another without getting her thoughts wet in the process. She was having an awkward time of it, partly because Diane Johnson of *New West* was already hanging on to Mr. Thomas's Epic for dear life, just daring anyone to challenge her possessive ecstasy: "A great book...with Freud and the Holocaust and the erotic dreamings of a young woman," sang Ms. Johnson girlishly, keeping her head just above water: "a celebration of human consciousness and of the unconscious." "Very likely the best book to appear in 1981," snorted Ensign Prescott of *Newsweek*; "Heartstunning," gasped Lehmann-Haupt of the *Times*; "I had found the book that would explain us to ourselves," sobbed Mr. Lehmann-Haupt's colleague Leslie Epstein, perhaps saying just a bit more than he'd intended to say. "Passionate, lyrical excess," panted young James Wolcott of *Esquire*, his little literary thighs pumping furiously as he tried (uncharacteristically) to keep up with the swim team. "A novel of erotic invention," thundered *New York* magazine, which had begun to take on water at an alarming rate. "Brutally explicit," promised the Book-of-the-Month Club. "Towers over virtually every other English-language work of fiction in the last two years," gasped *Publishers Weekly* weakly, and then everybody went under for the first time. They bobbed back up again, but they were beginning to look pretty soggy.

Perhaps the most reluctant seaman was poor John Updike of the *New Yorker*. Mr. Updike was, in the words of the publisher William Targ, "a talented and horny novelist," and the nation's "best purveyor of literary sexuality." For twenty years the Purveyor's feverish little novels of illicit sexual activity in the wilds of lower-middle-class New England had dominated the coffee-table pornography market (coffee-table porn usually consisted of about twenty-five pages of the hardcore stuff prettied up with several chapters of unusually dainty reviewer's prose), and now this horrible middle-aged Brit was horning in on the carefully cultivated territory without so much as a by-your-leave. What to do, what to do? Well, Mr. Updike knew when to pour scorn and when to go with the flow, and he started paddling fast, leaving huge spots of the most dreadful Updike-fluid behind him: "Thomas brings to the art of fiction a plenitude of feeling and ambition [be nice, John], and an ardent, generalizing approach...like little else in England or America," buzzed the New Yorker, proving that he hadn't been paying a whole lot of attention to the course of Anglo-American literature in recent years.

Some scholars of the period have insisted that John Updike wouldn't have known genuine human "feeling" if it had jumped out at him and squashed his Literary Sexuality, but it seems an irrelevant point: what *was* relevant, from Mr. Updike's somewhat suffocating perspective, was that Mr. Thomas's efforts had a "forthright sexuality," just like Mr. Updike's, and great dollops of "healthy sex" to boot (not to mention, God help us, one more "mythical earth mother" and "an unusual and exalting concern with paradise and with healing"). All the other fifty-year-old Purveyors at the writers' conferences were diving headfirst into Mr. Thomas's dollops of Healthy Sex, and John had to dive too, or be left to fade away in the backwash. Ergo, he just couldn't decide which of Mr. Thomas's products he liked best: the one with the character who was "first met

a week after his wife has bitten off his foreskin in a rage"
(Mr. Updike had a *special* fondness for scenes of a
certain type), or the one with the "long erotic sequence
involving images of Vietnam" (Vietnam had been ever
so sexy for some middle-aged writers who'd enjoyed the
war in the literary salons of Manhattan and London), or
the one with the even longer "erotic poem," or perhaps
...well, my goodness, they were *all* so exciting, he just
couldn't make up his mind! Mr. Thomas's next ship-
ment "should be an occasion," chanted Mr. Updike,
wagging his intellectual parts and praying, presumably, that he'd said the right thing.

It was a sweaty performance, made even less attractive
by its labored preciosity. It was, in other words, the sort
of performance one would have expected from John
Updike. (Let us remember that the one-word title of one
of Mr. Updike's own poems was, according to William
Targ, the plural form of a four-letter word used, in
literary circles, to describe the external female reproduc-
tive organs. The poem began with the line, "The Venus
de Milo didn't have one, at least no pussy," and crawled
through phrases like "I pulled a Tampax with my
teeth." Cute.) On the other hand, it must be said that the
linguistic whimpers and the emotional uglinesses of
the Updikes and the Thomases and their peers were the
consequence not of extreme stupidity or wickedness,
but of confusion and uncertainty and genuine fear.
While they may have been mean-spirited people, they
were not unintelligent people, or illiterate people; on
the contrary, some of them—most notably Mr.
Updike—were perfectly capable of arranging words
quite prettily, and sometimes took the trouble to do so.

And that is precisely the point: the kids were such ugly phrase-makers (and worshippers of other ugly phrase-makers) not because they lacked average skill, or education, or amiability, but because they had nothing better to do with themselves—because they were so bewildered by, and devoid of, serious mental or spiritual activity or aspiration. The rampant literary sleaziness—and make no mistake about it, we are talking about some pretty tacky humans—was almost accidental, a byproduct of institutionalized vacuity and timidity. Writers with nothing to write about invariably start covering themselves up with sex and gore, if only because they realize, almost instinctively, that those two subjects can be described and *understood* by otherwise hollow people.

The hollowness was the key. It—and by "it" we mean the vacuous uglinesses of the Updikes and the Thomases and their fellows—was the inevitable fruit of the union of cultural democracy and widespread spiritual decay. Indeed, the dark age had been forecast in great detail by many of the truest and most far-sighted prophets of the previous century. Writing in his journal a few years before his death, a very old Thomas Carlyle saw the beginnings of the plague of emptiness as "a very serious omen." Some few souls were beginning to do battle with their own "poor, bewildered hearts," to deny their knowledge of the human spirit, to persuade themselves that "virtue, vice are a *product*, like vitriol, like vinegar; this, and in general that human virtue is rotten, and all our high beliefs and aspirations *mud*!" In those pre-Updike days, the concept was still shocking, hard to grasp. But Carlyle grasped it, and saw where it would lead within fifty years, when "most or all" men and women would have succumbed to the plague: "There will be seen for some length of time (perhaps for several generations) such a world as few are dreaming of. But I never dread their 'abolition' of what is the Eternal *Fact* of *Facts*, and can prophecy that mankind generally will *return* to that with new clearness and sacred purity of zeal, or else perish utterly in unimaginable depths of anarchic misery and baseness.... But how deep are we to go? Through how many centuries, how many abject generations will it probably last?"

Fifty years later, the long night had begun. When Dean Inge described the progress of the disease in 1924, he spoke in ecclesiastical terms, but he meant to say what Carlyle had said:

> It would be a bold saying, that all great poets have seen life and Nature under the form of eternity; but if we understand eternity as the unchanging spiritual background of all experience, I think the statement might be defended.... The strange ebullition of utterly depraved art and literature, which, it must be remembered, is a European, not only a British disease, seems to be caused by the loss of spiritual standards reverenced by all. There are fundamental principles which were once under the keeping of a great religion, which in its highest forms brought all human life into a grand and beautiful harmony. This religion has now been rejected by the majority, who have no philosophy, no discipline, to put in its place. Ever since 1789, there has been an anarchic movement in European society, uprooting men from the soil on which their families had lived for centuries, and leaving them to drift rudderless upon the stormy sea of a chaotic civilization.

The retreat from civilization was by definition a retreat to emotional and intellectual primitivism. If the Updikes spent much of their time chattering away for the television cameras and telling reporters about their dreary private lives and attending writers' conferences and signing petitions and posing for pictures, rather than writing and thinking, they did so partly because they understood, on some unconscious level, that their fans did not value them as writers or thinkers, but as tribal priests—as medicine men who existed primarily in order to give their followers something to talk about. The whole game was an elaborate exercise designed to secure intellectual sanction for hundreds of individual emptinesses and for collective moral bankruptcy. Which is just another way of saying that hollow people write hollow books for hollow critics.

As for D.M. Thomas himself, he had seen the future, and the future was called America. He accepted an invitation from the chairman of the Literature Department of American University to teach "creative writing" in the New World. The chairman of the Literature Department in question was a man named Barry Chabot, and for reasons best left unexplored, he was anxious to expose his undergraduates to Mr. Thomas's tender fantasies. Perhaps the literary Mr. Chabot suspected, deep in his heart, that Mr. Thomas wouldn't have recognized real "Literature" (which even the Jacobin William Godwin had accepted as "the line of demarcation between the human and the animal kingdoms") if he'd fallen over it on his way to a literary awards ceremony, or perhaps Mr. Chabot just didn't have much time for careful reading, what with morning classes and all. In any case, Literature didn't really enter into it: what American University wanted was a Starlet, and preferably an erotic one.

The University got what it so desperately wanted, and what it so richly deserved. As soon as Mr. Thomas arrived in the States (in 1981), he began entertaining the literary campfollowers with appropriate stories. He told them all the things they'd hoped he would tell them. You know, book-talk: he told them, for instance, that (in the words of one interviewer) he "lived with one ex-wife," and that he "spent time with another," and he told them all about his literary struggles: "My second marriage was really a matter of legitimizing the child. My girlfriend and I wanted a child, but we really didn't want to be married.... The normal traumas of marriage and divorce didn't apply. It's a very cool thing." He spoke of his early work ("I wrote one about taking Princess Margaret to the movies and fondling her in the back row"), and he spoke of his family ("there was a familial eroticism probably due to my beloved sister in that period.... I'm sure that I conceived romantic or sexual fantasies about her"), and he spoke of—sorry— his "wet dreams." He wrote a review in which he expressed dislike for a character in a Saul Bellow novel ("the book suffers from his total decency") and he hinted at the rationale behind his own work: "It's very difficult to make virtue interesting." And finally he hummed an odd tune about the Agony of Creation:

> The book, when you write it, is a virgin. And then if it's produced in a mass marketing way, it obviously loses its virginity....When I see it now, it is up to a point a *product*....And maybe in 20 years

some poor student who has never heard of it will
buy a second-hand copy and be moved by it.

It was a sexy threat, in some eyes, but it was also a
hollow one. D.M. Thomas's books wouldn't be "moving" poor students "in 20 years," because Mr. Thomas
had already lost his moving license. Which is to say that
he was fast becoming old-hat, even as he droned on
about what should have been his private life. That is the
fate of the literary shocker, the professional insulter of
public opinion: in the very act of violating the conventions of decency and civility, he renders himself obsolete
and somewhat quaint. Defined by the conventions he
seeks to wreck, he destroys himself as he destroys the
social fabric that gave him identity in the first place.
The swarms of literary critics and obedient readers who
had given Mr. Thomas his moment in the sun had been
more than happy to do the ritual dances around the fire
at the moment of violation, but soon they would be
ready to move on, in search of more titillating kicks and
more outrageous—and younger—medicine men. The
American poet Longfellow explained the principle:
"Many readers judge of the power of a book by the
shock it gives their feelings;—as some savage tribes
determine the power of their muskets by the recoil; that
being considered best which fairly prostrates the pur-
chaser."

Armchair Shockers

Mr. Thomas's circumstances were not unique. Much
of the hysteria in the artistic community in the early

1980s was directly related to the growing realization that the community as a whole had lost its power to horrify the citizens. The approaching storm was, in large measure, a storm not of outrage, but of massive boredom. The community had always prided itself—and based its reputation—on its ability to cause a scene, to incite at least one literary riot in each fiscal quarter. The new threat of widespread calm was an unexpected one, and there were no contingency plans. The front-line troops—the aging middlebrowed reviewers, veterans of the Styron riot and the Doctorow bash and the Vonnegut battle and the Mailer party—tried to defend themselves against the forces of apathy by repeating the ritual shrieks of wilder times; but the voices were old and scratchy, and casualties were heavy.

There were pitiful squawks of "splendid" from John Leonard of the *New York Times* as he threw himself at Joyce Carol Oates's latest horror story, and echoes from the 1960s as Sylvia Martin of the *Chicago Sun-Times* got there first: "Love tender and love violent, murders and disappearances," chanted Ms. Martin, trying to drown out the ominous sound of the surf. "The supernatural, the bizarre, the grotesque, lyric pause and explosive horror... Enjoy!" "Voluptuously written," squealed John Calvin Batchelor of the *Village Voice*, just before the storm hit. After that all was chaos, and it was no longer possible to discover just which critics were making the most definitive statements about which Voluptuous Grotesqueries. The incessant gibberish had become one long rumble in the night, and Major Critics bobbed like corks in a sea of splendid horror.

Calm came with the dawn, and so too the Spirit of Riots Past, in the person of Jack Kroll of *Newsweek*. Mr. Kroll had attached his artistic conscience to the most decrepit intellectual craft he could find, and he was paddling dispiritedly about in extraordinarily stagnant waters, trying to interest the water-treaders in still another revival of a very bad old shocker from 1896, a play called *Ubu Roi*. Mr. Kroll thought that the crumbling atrocity had been written by "a snotty genius" (in fact it had been written by a psychologically disturbed French teenager), and he was pretty sure that it was "the most exciting and provoking event of the theater season." It was another of his favorite "epoch-making scandals of Western theater" (Hot Stuff, he meant), and it was so terribly Provoking that its first audience had been "outraged" at the deliciously "profane and scatological language." "It was a riot," sighed Mr. Kroll, who was understandably disappointed that no one could "recapture that sense of shock for a modern audience."

The gentleman from *Newsweek* could talk that way in his sleep. In the old days, the unsavory act had brought him what he so desperately wanted, attention. When he had said back in 1968 that "the only trouble" with a new show was that "its vaunted nude flash-scene" was "not lit well enough to really see this fleshly manifesto of the beautiful young people who give their all as no Broadway cast has ever done before," he had revealed some embarrassing things about himself, but he had also offended a few nice people, which was of course his purpose. That purpose hadn't changed in twelve years, but the nice people (and the not-so-nice people) had long ago moved on to other matters, and nobody seemed to be paying much attention to the old act.

Still, Mr. Kroll was going to do his best. The new production managed to turn "grossness and brutish-ness into an inside-out grace," and that was what The Theatre was all about, my dears: you know, "dynamit-ing the complacent hypocrisy of society's dead center," and sticking your tongue out at "the authority figures of the graying and self-satisfied bourgeoisie," and all the other intellectual activities that had kept so many literary reputations afloat for so many dreary years. And still nobody seemed very interested. "If I were you, I'd stick that ass of yours on a throne" scribbled Mr. Kroll, almost doubling up with helpless literary laughter. That, he explained, was one of his favorite lines from *Ubu Roi*, spoken by the "shrewd and lewd pussycat, a gutter-talking Lady Macbeth." Still no response. Well, "language really doesn't matter," said Mr. Kroll quickly. What the play was *really* "telling" him was that "real understanding comes from the total expressiveness of people vibrating in the throes of passion or obsession," okay?

For reasons best known to the editors of *Newsweek*, Jack Kroll never did get around to quoting the play's most unforgettable lines: "Fart, s--t, it's hard to get him moving, but fart, s--t, I reckon I've shaken him all the same. Thanks to God and myself, in a week, maybe, I'll be Queen of Poland." Mr. Kroll, it seemed, was another armchair shocker, meek as a mouse when it came to the pages of his own magazine. Not at all like the brave little worker who'd directed the obscene schoolboy farce: *he* was "the most undoubted genius of Western directors." Oddly enough, the Undoubted Genius had a sneaking feeling that there was "something profoundly wrong with Western society," something which only *Ubu* could cure. Even so—and not surprisingly—the UG was "not particularly interested in theater or art as such": "I'm like a volcanologist who goes from volcano to volcano, looking for the biggest eruption," he admitted, as if it needed saying. Mr. Kroll tried to put the best possible face on his idol's confessions: "He's turned away in order to point the way," said the critic vaguely, hoping that no one would ask him for directions.

He needn't have worried: he was speaking only to himself and a few of his close friends. And he seemed disheartened. "Why should he [the Undoubted Genius] not deal with those muggers he speaks of who are in even worse spiritual shape?" pouted Mr. Kroll, sticking out his literary lip. "We cannot tell our best artists what path to follow," and *anyway*, "we need him to generate and regenerate our own lives upon his stage, the most brilliant stage of our lifetime." If Mr. Kroll didn't actually stamp his little foot, surely it was only because he suspected that the framework of his intellectual lifeboat wouldn't have held up under the sudden pressure.

Not that he was about to give up without a fight. After all, he had the Royal Shakespeare Company's new play about the pop singer Edith Piaf in his pocket. *That* would show them. "The profanity and some scatological scenes will shock some people," promised poor Mr. Kroll, with just a hint of the old spirit. Listen, he said, leaning closer: "When Piaf, grinning like a mischievous child, seems to urinate on stage, this isn't the bland titillation we get from a Rona Barrett." It was *much* better titillation than that: it was the "mocking, indecorous pugnacity of a wounded street animal who was born to snarl but learned to sing," so could we keep it, Mom, *please?* Mr. Kroll didn't have time to explain why he associated public micturition with "titillation" (not to mention Rona Barrett), but it was decided that he could keep his stray plays if he would remember to spread fresh newspaper on the deck every morning (or perhaps some old theater criticism from *Newsweek*).

Momentarily encouraged, the indefatigable critic tried to bring himself up to date with an old John Osborne play from the beloved 1960s. It was "lacerating and truth-telling," hissed Mr. Kroll, with an inviting literary gesture. He promised a "terrible black hole of moral collapse," and one of the "most brutally demanding roles of the modern stage"; also a lovely "portrait of a man flayed down to the raw jelly of self-loathing and guilt—a portrait of a spiritual suicide whom we recognize with a shock as our brother." Everybody traded nervous glances and tried to paddle away from Mr. Kroll's 1960s boat: the damn thing just didn't look very safe anymore. It looked downright nasty, in a childish sort of way.

Mr. Kroll tried to look a bit more trendy. "If the British playwrights of the '50s and '60s were Angry Young Men," he said, "then those of the '70s and '80s are Furious." Mr. Kroll said that he had found some new playwrights who had "a new passion," and he swore up and down that the playwrights had "often discomfited and shocked audiences." "From sex to

socialism," said the critic, trying to ignore the yawns.
"From economics to anxiety," he whispered, sounding
a bit anxious himself. Mr. Kroll had one dear little play
called *Slag*, and another called *Knuckles*, which was
about a "sensational rape case": it went From Sex to
Socialism, of course, but it also went "from pop to
philosophy." And don't go away, please don't go away,
he had another one that went "from empire to impotence" and "from order to confusion." Look here, look
here, he had the same old cast of characters with him, all
your old favorites: there was the guy who had "geriatric
sex with his housekeeper," and there was the "hint of
incest and even murder," and look over there, why there
was the familiar old "corruption of a society that has
touched moral bottom." Didn't that just take you back a
few years!

But by this time it was obvious that Mr. Kroll had just
slapped a new coat of gore onto the same old 1960s
rowboat, and nobody was falling for it. The critic began
to sound a bit panicky: the playwrights would play
"clever games with the audience," he said; there would
be "a naked, blood-smeared man on a bed," there would
be a girl who would "end her relationship with her
unsuccessful impregnator by emptying a revolver in his
direction," and dammit, what was the matter with everybody? Where was everybody going? These plays were
"meaningful," shouted Mr. Kroll. "It's this kind of
creative youth," he roared, "that is shaping the future of
the American theater." But he was all alone in his tiny
boat, going around and around in little circles in the
middle of a stagnant pond, mocked by the echo of his
own obsolete catechism.

Buzzing

One who stood and watched was Edith Milton of *New York* magazine. Like Doris Grumbach, Ms. Milton was a former Information Officer who had moved over to the Office of Motivation and Instruction without abandoning her easily imitable style in the process. Ms. Milton was trying to dry off the stories of Nadine Gordimer (which weren't all that wet to begin with), because "what motivates these stories" was "a profound consciousness of the strength of the insane systems by which society tries to protect its own interests, and a celebration of everything that refuses to be instructed by them or contained in their deadly limits." It went without saying that Ms. Gordimer's "fine and tragic vision" looked "on a time and place where no one wins, where love is the beginning of betrayal and peace merely the starting point of hostility," and that kind of thing. And if one heard a few buzzes as the words trickled by, it was only because they had trickled by in such similar fashion so many times before.

They were very like the words that the kids from *Saturday Review* liked to dump all over the novels of Graham Greene, for example: "Books may mean what they say, and they may mean lots of other things; in this context, writer and reader become spies together, practicing for their difficult life in the world, juggling their double allegiance to an innocence that is not always an illusion and to a suspicion that is not always justified." And they were very like the words that trickled by when the omnipresent Jack Kroll of *Newsweek* went to see an adaptation of an old play by Frank Wedekind, a play that had thrilled the Krolls of 1904 because it had, in the late Jacob Hartmann's words, "gone further in depicting the unsavory side of sex relations than any other play in literature." Presumably Mr. Kroll was unfamiliar with Jacob Hartmann, because he was still being thrilled in the 1980s: the play, he said, constituted a "vision of woman as man's fantasy struggling to become her own reality."

There it was again: "reality." Mr. Kroll's entire career had been built, like so many others, on his ability to cover himself up with the twin blankets of "reality" and "fantasy" whenever the going got tough and unsavory. He had been under his covers ever since 1973, when he had been scared by a great big play that had "characterized with subversive logic" the "shadow between illusion and reality" and the "torturous tension between fantasy and reality that modern man [for "modern man" read "Jack Kroll"] must maintain." (Of the same 1973 production, a more courageous critic from *Time* magazine—Richard Schickel—had said, "Who, then, is sane? Who is crazy? Who cares?") And now Mr. Kroll was back at the same old stand, primarily because it had become the only stand in town; and just as he'd been afraid that "purists" would reject the "high voltage of reality" that characterized his "Hamlet-champion," so was he afraid that "purists" would mock the "high-voltage exchange of energy" that marked the "vision of woman as man's fantasy struggling to become her own reality."

And yet Mr. Kroll knew Reality when he saw it, that's what frustrated him so: Reality was "the modern world," the "maddening melange of beauty and trash, promise and perversion," and the Wedekind play *had* it, damn it, complete with "cheap hooker," "punkish rock star," "Son of Sam-type killer," "incestuous foster father," "lesbian lover," and all the rest of the familiar crew. It was all just too, too "contemporary," or so Mr. Kroll kept telling himself. There was an especially kicky scene in which "art miscegenates with fashion," or something, and then there were all those "shifting levels of action that dislocate the perspective with dizzying effect," and all in all it was exactly the sort of dizzying reality that got Mr. Kroll all—well, all dizzy. Mr. Kroll's final artistic perspective was about as large as a suburban movie theater: just as the fight scenes in his favorite *Hamlet* were almost as good as the fights Mr. Kroll had seen on the really big screen, so did the "flow and drive" of the current production make "most movies look static." Why, the whole drama was "challenging" the audience with "the most inventive and exciting" play Mr. Kroll had seen that year, and he was all giggly inside, just like old times: "The viewers are either outraged or bowled over," he said hopefully, and Outraging and Bowling Over was "exactly what a live contemporary theater is all about."

And so it was. It was for precisely that reason that "live contemporary theater," as Mr. Kroll understood it, had become an anachronism. It was for precisely that reason that Mr. Kroll's creaky enthusiasms—and his ritualistic language—had become so musty with the telltale odor of the anxious shocker who can no longer shock. Audiences just didn't want to be bowled over or buzzed at or outraged by Mr. Kroll and his playmates anymore. Everybody had been very polite about the whole thing for years, but they had also been secretly bored: if the kids couldn't learn to behave like little grownups when they were in the parlor, then it was time for them to go upstairs and shut the door behind them. There was going to be some grown-up talk.

The language of Kroll and Grumbach—which is to say, the language of the expiring literary establishment—was the language of childhood precisely because it was the language of pretension: as a child will parrot the words of his or her parents without knowing what they mean, so did the cultural stragglers continue to repeat the phrases that had always sounded most important to their ears. They had become an interest group battling for a share of influence, seeking to preserve their sense of self-importance by bullying an increasingly disgusted public into extending their mandate for another decade or two. The more they were called to account, the louder did they howl; the more they were asked to explain what they knew of art, the more did they inflate their language and disguise their lack of discipline. They spoke of "renewing one's sense of the possibilities of prose," of "illuminating the human condition," of "speaking to the humanity in us all"; and when they couldn't come up with a suitably amorphous buzz, they italicized an inappropriate verb or two as a show of lazy sincerity: "They express a robust joy in the thorough *doing* of a tale" (Walter Clemons, *Newsweek*).

But it had all been going on for too many years. When John Leonard of the *New York Times* said that a dreary novel of political scatology from Joseph Heller "requires us to revise our own imaginations," nobody wanted to revise. When Mr. Leonard told *Esquire* that he always read Colman McCarthy's columns because "whatever he wants to think about, I'm willing to think about in his prose rhythms," it was no longer precociously cute, it was just sticky—and it was sticky largely because it didn't mean anything. When Anatole Broyard of the *New York Times* said that the novelist John Casey was "equally good in describing the grandeur and the dandruff of the self," many readers thought vaguely of the new biotin shampoos before turning the page. And when Brendan Gill of the *New Yorker* said of one of Mr. Casey's erotic sagas that it showed "precisely how contemporary young people—a generation of passionate truth-tellers—respond to the sometimes delectable, sometimes anguished ripening of their bodies and minds," it was not just funny, it was genuinely embarrassing. It became more than embarrassing as the sixty-year-old Gill continued: "In and out of bed," giggled the veteran New Yorker, "how enviable his characters are in their determination to fulfill themselves!" Oh Good Lord Mr. Gill was trying to fulfill himself: "Hearing those voices, one would give anything to join them."

And so it went, from absurdity to embarrassment to excruciating boredom. As the American essayist Christian Bovee said, paraphrasing Swift: "There are few wild beasts more to be dreaded than a communicative man having nothing to communicate." So it was that when Larzer Ziff of *Commonweal* praised William Styron's latest effort on the grounds that it "asserted art's power and thus art's right to break in upon even sacred silence," it was no longer a scary peek at literary misconceptions about the rights of power, it was just deadly party talk. By the same token, when President Carter handed Eudora Welty a Medal of Freedom and told her that she had "illuminated the human condition," it didn't affect her reputation one way or the other. She didn't even bother to deny the accusation. And when a reviewer for the Book-of-the-Month Club said that Mordecai Richler's latest Memorable Novel was "life-affirming," it was no longer merely a silly phrase, it was actually offensive, intellectually and otherwise—and part of the reason it was offensive was that Mordecai Richler was a member of the Editorial Board of the Book-of-the-Month Club. Communicative men with nothing to communicate end up speaking to and about themselves: by 1980, the language of pretension existed for no other reason than to exalt itself, and thereby its practitioners.

The empty words were a defense against thought, because thought was the final enemy. Unabashed intellect, whatever its conclusions, seemed to terrify the members of the community, perhaps because it required them to react in an equally straightforward way. It was better that profundity be...hinted at. So that the participants might speak of horrors that were "ultimately affirmative," of writers and painters and musicians who implied that "guilt is the bond that makes humanity human," of philosophers who "transcended nothingness." It was the language of evasion, and the trick—the only vital trick—was to avoid the direct statement. The idea was abroad in the frightened world that the direct and lucid expression of complex thought was somehow...somehow unsophisticated. It would get you into trouble, make an easy target of you. They might try to say what they meant in Hoboken, but here, by God, we had learned to walk in the shadows, to hint softly through half-closed lips; and if there was less meaning than met the ear, or no meaning at all, we did not want to know about it.

Chapter VIII

The Cultural Democracy

Cultural work was easy work, and it was not surprising that everybody wanted a piece of the action. By the end of the 1970s, every idle college instructor in the land had collaborated on at least one innovative novel of scatology, every bubbly local activist had treated the community to a one-man or one-woman show at the local gallery, every bored graduate student had become the most important artist of his or her generation.

And why not? There were no entrance requirements, beyond a basic ability to arrange words or notes or colors in a reasonably imaginative way, and the pay was okay. It was not hard to write as well as or better than Vonnegut or Oates or Dickey or Beattie or any one of a thousand garrulous children of the electronic age; it was a snap to duplicate or improve upon the sounds of early Foss or the visions of late Calder; it was but the work of a moment to outdistance the Grumbachs and the Leonards and the Krolls and the Kaels in their aimless raptures over random Illuminations of the Human Condition and incessant Affirmations of Life. By 1980, there were at least two artists in every garage and a philosopher in every pot. The museum basements were clogged with interchangeable twentieth-century masterworks, the library floors were piled high with last week's dazzling erotic epics, the theaters were thick with thousands of rudderless critics, the airwaves were cacophonous with the meaningless gobbles of cut-out intellectuals and apprentice pundits; and still the stuff came spewing out. There was just no more room for all the genius: the citizenry was gagging as it tried to force the increasingly unpalatable debris down its own throat, and the cultural community was slowly choking to death on the fruits of its own democratization. What Carlyle had foreseen in the summer of 1867 had finally come to pass, with a vengeance:

> Only wait: in fifty years, I should guess, all really serious souls will have quitted that mad province [of art], left it to the roaring populaces; and for any *Noble* man or useful person it will be a credit rather to declare, "I never tried Literature; believe me, I have not written anything!"

Everybody knew that something was horribly, horribly wrong, but it was the nature of the disease that nobody in charge had any idea what it was. Indeed, editors and museum directors and publishers were particularly hard hit, and particularly bewildered. "Here we sit," said the fiction editor of the *Minnesota Review*: "small publication, don't pay anything, no fame—and in the last month before our deadline for the fiction issue, we received about three hundred stories, perhaps fifty good ones and a couple of dozen very good ones. Where are all those people? Who's reading them? Whom are they writing for?'' The problem, of course, was not so much that the editor of the *Minnesota Review* had received three hundred stories, but that the editor of the *Minnesota Review* actually thought that fifty of the stories were "good," and that twenty-four of them were "very good." Not just literate, or readable—but very good.

It was an absurdity that could only have been uttered by a man in his "profession": no military commander would have been silly enough to imply that there were fifty men in the outfit who would make good generals, no professor of biology would have risked his scientific reputation by saying that there were fifty future prize-winners among his students, or even among all the students in the country. The difference between the average biologist and the average writer or editor was that the biologist still remembered (a) what he was supposed to be doing, (b) why he was doing it, and (c) how he would be able to tell whether he had done it or not. The dilemma of the cultural establishment was the dilemma of the biologist who has been told that because biology is an inexact science, all scientific procedures have been abolished, and that henceforth all prizes are to be awarded by lottery.

That was the dilemma Jay Neugeboren was up against when he edited a special issue of *Ploughshares* magazine, an issue devoted entirely to fiction. Writing in the *Nation*, Mr. Neugeboren said that he'd received more than nine hundred submissions, and that "within the first six weeks, when I'd read perhaps fifty manuscripts, I could have put together an issue of a dozen stories that I would have been proud of and whose quality would have been, in my opinion, superior to most issues of *Story*, and equal to the general level of recent volumes of *Best Stories*." Poor Mr. Neugeboren still had five months and eight hundred and fifty manuscripts to go: in the end, he didn't even bother to open the last five hundred envelopes. There was desperation in the air: "*Where*, I kept asking myself—and others—*were all these good writers coming from*, and who were they? Why were there so many good stories looking for a home?... Why...did these writers keep writing? Why did they keep submitting?"

Mr. Neugeboren's problem was the curse of the community, and one of the hidden sources of all the panic: "I had to make choices, and I was reading many stories that, though I didn't especially *like* them, were clearly well written, original, sometimes dazzling. Were some of these stories nevertheless deserving of publication, because they were so accomplished, even though they did not especially appeal to me?" The poor chap didn't *know*, you see, he didn't know how to tell whether something was good or not, how to tell whether it was "deserving" of publication or not: all he had to go on were some vague sensations of "liking" or "disliking," but he didn't really know why he liked or disliked. For all he knew, maybe *everything* was "deserving" of publication: after all, there were no rules, were there? It was art, wasn't it? And art was...art was...art was art, or something.

Mr. Neugeboren was a well-intentioned man, and his confusion was understandable, if not harmless. All he wanted to know was, How could you tell? How *did* one define the difference between mediocrity and genius, between professionalism and talent, between entertainment and art: how did one know where and when to make the assumption of significance? If styles had become interchangeable, if the overt expression of intellect was an embarrassment, if ethical conclusions were disallowed—how could you tell?

Mr. Neugeboren solved his immediate problem in the same way that most of his colleagues had solved theirs: he decided to approve stories that were about "loss, exile, displacement," though he did not say what he meant by the redundant trinity, nor why stories that embodied it were particularly "deserving of publication." It was just that these exile-stories "moved" Mr. Neugeboren, and "drove" him. They were "central" to, um, "something" in Mr. Neugeboren, and he was willing to "trust" that "centrality," which was also a "sensibility." And a damn good thing, too, or he'd have had to open the other five hundred envelopes and the issue still wouldn't be on the stands.

Mr. Neugeboren had a lot in common with Stanley Elkin, the editor of *The Best American Short Stories 1980*, who concluded in desperation that "taste is, finally, a series of first impressions, lodestar aesthetics that last a lifetime." Why heck, Mr. Elkin told an interviewer, "it may even be one of the famous drives, like sex or appetite." He explained, or tried to explain, what he was talking about: "My mother-in-law would be incapable of furnishing a living room without slipcovers, and, for her, the development of clear plastic was a technological breakthrough, a hinge event in science, up there with washable mah-jongg tiles." In the clear plastic tradition, Mr. Elkin had been Informing his own taste—listening to a pop record called *Neil Diamond's Greatest Hits*—when all of a sudden he thought, "Hey, this is terrific! I could put out a book called *Stanley Elkin's Greatest Hits!*" So, he did. When you're in touch with your lodestar aesthetics, editing a book is but the work of a moment, and Mr. Elkin finished the job "rather hurriedly"—in one day, actually. "But hell," concluded the aesthete, "I'm pretty satisfied with it." But then, how did he know he was satisfied? How could he tell? How could anybody tell?

In the eleventh hour, the New York Times Book Company addressed itself to a trembling community. "What you need," thundered the Company, "is a team of experts with impeccable taste who can *unerringly* steer you to the winners and keep you from the losers." The Company had just the experts for an ailing nation, and by a happy coincidence they all worked for the *New York Times*: "See how Anatole Broyard, Christopher Lehmann-Haupt, John Leonard and other respected literati rate the new releases," said the publishers, spinning the wheel of chance. All the "much-quoted critics" who were "acknowledged" to be "among the most authoritative in the nation" were going to do their bit and "provide their final word on the blockbusters—and the bombs." After all, there were tough times ahead, and the community was going to have to hang together if it was to survive at all. "Even if you don't find time to read the book, you'll learn enough to navigate success-

fully at the most 'glamorous' cocktail party," promised
the Company.

It was an indication of the extent of the demoraliza-
tion that the admen were willing to drop all the old
façades and come right out in front of everybody with
the bit about the cocktail parties. But then, perhaps the
Company was only trying to catch up with the *New
York Review of Books*, which was making a big dent in
the cultural cocktail market by offering partygoers a
"specially designed bookbag of heavy navy blue canvas
with beige straps," sporting the "distinctive *New York
Review* logo." It would hold "books, French bread, a
bottle of wine, and the *New York Review*." Not that
there was anything especially unpleasant about a navy
blue canvas bookbag with beige straps. Unfortunately,
this particular navy blue canvas bookbag with beige
straps featured a "caricature of Shakespeare, also in
beige," and there *was* something unpleasant about that.
There was something deadly about that.

The *New York Review* and the *New York Times* were
announcing, somewhat belatedly, what had been
embarrassingly clear to the rest of the world for a long
time: that the literary community was not, in fact, a
particularly bookish community. It had been years
since the blue-bagging literary partygoers had actually
bothered to read one another's dreary publications, just
as it had been years since any of them had actually acted
upon a real idea (let alone ordered their lives upon one).
Books were not for reading, and ideas were not a basis
for life: books were for talking and shouting about, and
an idea was something you passed around with the

pistachios and the burnt peanuts, until you grew tired of sniffing at it (after which it became something you had "been through"). This would have been fine (given the quality of the books and the childishness of the ideas), had it not been for all the worthy writers who were being ignored or shoved into the corner in the process: all the writers who were more interested in being read than in being talked about, who exhibited an eccentric desire to write sentences and paragraphs rather than Bombs and Blockbusters.

If the aging literary butterflies had been paying more attention to where their anti-intellectualism was taking them, they wouldn't have been getting in the way of grown-up folk like J.I.M. Stewart and Gabriel Fielding and Evelyn Page and Gerald Warner Brace and Lord Blake and Lady Snow and Fred Uhlman and Michael Campbell and John E. Mack and Leslie Croxford and Roger Cleeve and...well, anyone who actually reads books can complete the list with his or her own choices, with the names of sharp and conscientious writers who were (and are) more interested in casting light than in precipitating a literary riot on the verandas of Nantucket or in the faculty lounges of New Jersey or southern California. These writers (and others like them) were possessed of varying degrees of grace and intelligence and perception and imagination and purpose, but all of them, at one level or another, had something grown-up to say; and—just as important—all of them wanted their readers to *understand* what they were saying. It followed that few of the honest names were household words, in 1980: genuine purpose is, after all, incompatible with panic—because panic itself is the enemy of historical, philosophical, and literary perspective. Said Ruskin: "In all the arts and acts of life, the secret of high success will be found, not in a fretful and various excellence, but in a quiet singleness of justly chosen aim." Voices worth listening to are often quiet voices, and quiet voices cannot easily be heard when a riot is in progress—or when a party is breaking up.

It has been our tendency, in many of these arguments, to concede the last word to the fellow who handed the banner to John Ruskin, Thomas Carlyle. The favoritism is deliberate: Carlyle was not only one of the last of the influential moral giants, standing like a beacon at the fatal intersection of human progress, lighting the way to the road not taken; he was also the most clear-eyed prophet of our present discontent. He was there when we took the wrong turning, and he warned of the spiritual and intellectual desert that we would find at the end of the road to cultural democracy.

The danger, as he saw it, was in the distraction: ordinary men and women turned to "art," and the worship of art, only when they had nothing more important to do or to think about. And idle humans—bored humans—were not whole humans. They were shells, chattering away to keep their spirits up as the sun went down. It was precisely because Carlyle believed that literature could be one of the worthiest human occupations, when pursued by men and women "whom nature had furnished gloriously for that task, like Goethe and Schiller," that he had so little use for the masses of self-proclaimed "artists" and "writers" who littered the intellectual landscape. He told his future biographer James Anthony Froude that the modern man of letters, the man or woman "who had turned to literature as a means of living, was generally someone who had gone into it because he was unfit for better work, because he was too vain or too self-willed to travel along the beaten highways, and his writings, unless he was one of a million, began and ended in nothing." "Life," he believed, "was action, not talk. The speech, the book, the review or newspaper article was so much force expended—force lost to practical usefulness. When a man had *uttered* his thoughts, still more when he was always uttering them, he no longer even attempted to translate them into act."

And yet Carlyle never doubted that humanity would eventually regain its balance. Froude again, with his acknowledgement of things that were and will be:

> He said once to me that England had produced her greatest men before she began to have a literature at all. Those Barons who signed their charter by dipping the points of their steel gauntlets in the ink, had more *virtue, manhood,* practical force and wisdom than any of their successors; and when the present disintegration had done its work, and healthy organic tissue began to form again, tongues would not chatter as they did now. Those only would speak who had call to speak.

Chapter IX

Death Ship

The dishonor was not in the confusion, but in the ritualistic character of that confusion; not in the appalling cultural, scientific, and historical ignorance, but in the refusal to mend that ignorance; not in the incompetence, but in the exaltation of that incompetence; not in the mediocrity of execution, but in the meanness of intention.

Long-running farce finally became intellectual tragedy when a wisely anonymous essayist at *Time* magazine pulled out all the stops and declared that the star of the science-fiction film *The Empire Strikes Back* was the "unpretentious cinematic heir" to such pretentious heroes as "Prometheus, Jason, Aeneas, Sir Galahad, John Bunyan's pilgrim." *The Empire Strikes Back* was, God help us, all about a Homeric hero "who ventures forth into dangerous and unknown territory, who is tempted by his own dark impulses, but who eventually conquers them and emerges victorious.'' ''The story thus symbolizes man's ability to control the irrational savage that exists within him,'' explained the philosopher from *Time*, trying very hard not to sound like an irrational savage, and incidentally spilling popcorn all over what he or she knew of the Homeric myths. *Time* was kind enough to say that ''the adventures of Luke Skywalker'' bore ''only a superficial resemblance to the quest of Homer's 'kingly man,' '' but typical enough to insist that both tales drew ''from the same deep wells of mythology, the unconscious themes that have always dominated history on the planet,'' harrumph. Which was exactly what one would have expected from the magazine that had helped to call the original party to order back in 1927 by announcing that the poet Robinson Jeffers ranked with ''Homer and Sophocles,'' and indeed with ''the greatest poets of all generations.'' All in all, it was not so surprising that the Homeric Age that had begun with Robinson Jeffers should end with Artoo Detoo. But there was shame in it.

To speak of this shame—to speak, that is, of a general artistic, intellectual, and cultural collapse—is really, as we have seen, to speak of a literary failure of almost unimaginable proportion. Genuine culture, like the men and women who possess it, may be timeless and enduring, but such culture is only as important (or as weak) in the life of a nation as the books and plays and magazines and newspapers that embody and distribute its values. Accordingly, while it is not expected of every age that it be capable of producing good art, it *is* demanded of the literary establishment of every age that it at least keep the memory and the standard of good art always before itself, well polished and clearly labeled. A literary establishment that cannot do this—which is to say, a literary establishment that does not know what art looks like—can only work with what happens to be lying around at the moment: such a community feeds only on itself, and dies as its members retire, leaving no cultural legacy.

That was the source of all the trouble in the early 1980s, of course: the halls were clogged with idle men and women who wanted desperately to read and write, and there were lots and lots of pens and typewriters—but there was nothing to write about. The hangers-on of the postwar cultural establishment, the pursed-lipped reviewers and the popular book clubs and the erotic periodicals, were still awake and kicking, albeit somewhat feebly, but the artists themselves—the once-powerful craftsmen and the once-influential thinkers—were no longer around to be worshipped. It was all over: from Havelock Ellis and Anaïs Nin to Shere Hite and Philip Roth, from Chatterley's loins to the dissonant chord, from Pablo and Papa and Alice B. to Miller and Mailer and Masters and Johnson, the names and noises and postures and visions that had defined the bizarre cult of the infantile for the greater part of the spiritually stagnant century had suddenly become targets for general intellectual ridicule and symbols of protracted cultural farce. Irreverent newcomers were trying to keep a straight face in front of the Vonneguts and the Jongs and the Warhols and the Doctorows, and yawning while the Mailers and the Capotes chattered on and on about Marilyn Monroe, and everywhere there was a sneaking fear that the half-century of aberrant art was going to turn out to be just that: an aberration.

It was this fear that was sparking the sillier manifestations of literary perversity and hysteria, as the intellectual beneficiaries of the postwar establishment, the third-generation pretenders and their aging attendants, began to suspect that they had missed the turning of the tide, and that their exposure was going to be a bitter one. Most knew that it was all over, but nobody wanted to say it, because nobody could afford to say it: there were long careers and swollen reputations at stake, and more than a few bucks as well. As the darkness closed in, everbody was still scribbling furiously, and the shell of the literary community still stood, apparently solid, like the hulk of a gutted ship. But there was no longer anybody in the engine room.

Interlude:

Clearing the Decks

"There is a law of neutralization of forces," said Lowell, "which hinders bodies from sinking beyond a certain depth in the sea; but in the ocean of baseness, the deeper we get, the easier the sinking."

What is manifestly true of the individual spirit is just as true of the occasional corpse of national character, or intellect, or culture (the crucial difference being that the individual must forever recall and enclose his iniquity within his remorse, whereas a people is always in a position to make itself clean again through its children, be they actual or spiritual; the individual regenerates and completes himself by making his own amends, but a civilization worthy of the name must assign to the sons and the daughters the task of atonement, in order that the bad may gradually weaken, and the memory of the good accumulate—to survive long after the civilization itself has surrendered). And so it was with the unpleasantly decrepit body of the Anglo-American cultural establishment. The awful pallbearers of the century's shabby legacy—the leering old critics and the ghastly old novelists and the obsequious executive editors and the finger-snapping academics and the sleazy book clubs and the computerized publishers—had guided their cadaverous vessel over their private "ocean of baseness" for so many tedious years that they could no longer remember where they had come from, or even why they had set out on the torturous voyage in the first place.

Unwilling to withdraw, however awkwardly, from the public scene (which would have been the first measure in the long procedure of atonement and repair), and unable to return to port, the shattered crew resolved to embrace the rising tides of outrageous fortune by throwing a series of diversionary tantrums.

In the weeks and months to come, the wretched representatives of the old order would seek to perpetuate their original error and evade the judgement of time by struggling almost obsessively against their unseen enemies (who turned out to be everybody who was or ever had been or ever would be on dry land), and against the increasingly remote possibility of rescue. In the process, they would seek to escape, and even revoke, the ineluctable truths of art and philosophy; they would despoil the meaning and negate the usefulness of the past with the confusions of the present; and before it was all over they would try to regain the attention (and the dollars) of their somnolent peers by taking off the last of their gaudy pretenses and doing the ancient bump and grind of the fading literary charlatan, right up there on the best-seller chart.

It would be a fleshy display of spiritual and intellectual flab such as had never been seen before and would quite possibly never be seen again in the gardens of the West, the final orgiastic blast of the period of suspended cultural adolescence that had been conceived in the 1890s, stroked and nurtured in the pause between the world wars, and finally honored in the chaos of the nuclear age. In indulging themselves in the final literary debauch, the Keepers of the Adolescence would abase their countrymen, gleefully demolish what remained of their own intellectual integrity and literary reputation, and finally deliver the body of the aberrant regime to the depths of the historical seas, bereft of even the little honor it had gathered unto itself in the dreary decades of moral flippancy and artistic deceit. The open-mouthed watchers on the shores of the real world would have found it hard to credit, at the time, but the most horrible acts of exhibitionism were still to come, in the final manic performance of the departing cultural administration; and the literary state of the English-speaking world was going to get much worse before it began—almost imperceptibly, at first—to get better.

Ahead lie monsters.

Chapter X

Savaging the Past

> And therefore here I stand forth, only to make good the place we have thus taken up, and to defend the sacred monuments erected therein, which contain the honour of the dead, the fame of the living, the glory of peace, and the best power of our speech; and wherein so many honourable spirits have sacrificed to memory their dearest passions, shewing by what divine influence they have been moved, and under what stars they lived.
>
> —Samuel Daniel, 1602

As the absence of any significant body of genuine contemporary art became increasingly difficult to ignore, there was the inevitable surge of resentment against the art of the past. Just as an unusually rudderless adolescent may seek to exalt his unfinished state—and postpone the years of social responsibility—by assaulting the values of maturity, so did the post-war cultural

118

establishment hope to maintain a shred of its former reputation—and delay the hour of accountability—by snapping at the authority of the ages.

It was an appalling spectacle, partly because the little snappers were so long past their own physical adolescence, and partly because they were so unabashed in the bitterness of their resentment: even the most anxious of youths will try to dignify his fear of adulthood with traditional arguments of political or social theory, but the cultural reactionaries of 1980 came right out in the open and scrawled their mean provincialism on the walls for all to see.

It was a form of literary exhibitionism made possible by ignorance but prompted by despair; and despair by its very nature is, as Montaigne's friend Charron said, "like forward children, who, when you take away one of their playthings, throw the rest into the fire for madness. It grows angry with itself, turns its own executioner, and revenges its misfortunes on its own head." Alas, it was not an establishment that cared much for Pierre Charron (or for Montaigne), and the assault on the past grew more insistent as the future grew more ominous: no one in a position of authority seemed to realize that each new attack of bitterness only peeled another layer from the intellectual reputation of the present, and stripped another hour or two from the final days of the gasping era.

Certainly they didn't realize it in the art department of the *New Republic*, where the critic John Canaday was charging through the corridors of beauty with a literary sledgehammer, taking wild swings at anything that smacked of nobility or purpose. First to fall was the

great cathedral at Amiens, which even the cautious
Ruskin had referred to as "the Parthenon of Gothic
architecture": it became, in Mr. Canaday's angry hands,
"the dullest of major medieval monuments." Encouraged by his easy victory, the seventy-three-year-old kill-
joy took a quick crack at one of the greatest of Renaissance painters—"it is safe for the first time in nearly five
centuries to find Raphael tiresome"—and set off down
the hall in search of Athens. When he arrived, he was
firm but cunning: "Nobody is discarding the Parthenon and the Elgin marbles," he said slyly—but let's
face it, Novelty was ever so much more exciting than
excellence, and "young classical scholars" would find
much "more excitement" in the "variety" and the
"wider range of humanistic attitudes" of later periods.
Suddenly Mr. Canaday spied a familiar giant in the
corner, and he lashed out: it was safe, he cried, "to
regard Michelangelo as more baroque (and what a dirty
word 'baroque' used to be) than golden." The triumphant critic surveyed the wreckage, and it was fine:
"Give it a little more time," he said anxiously, "and all
those golden ages may begin to look more like preludes
than consummations. Which would be all to the good."

But the sweet moment of hope was interrupted by an
awful scream from the other end of the campus, where
Henry James was receiving his lumps from the humanist Jonathan Yardley, one of the nation's leading book
critics. Mr. Yardley, a good man and true, was nevertheless complaining that James's novel *The Golden Bowl*
was a "boring" book, almost as boring as Henry
Adams's silly old autobiography. Damn straight, said
Mr. Yardley's editorial bosses at the *Washington Star*,

gleefully tossing Booth Tarkington into the trash (*Pen-rod and Sam* was "an artifice"), and incidentally expressing the fear that the new Faulkner Book Awards might become—what else—"a child of literary elit-ism." And if the Elitists were coming, could the Snobs and (shudder) the Purists be far behind?

There was a kind of perverse cyclical logic to all this: when the pack is in full retreat—when your local Lead-ing Critic is ill at ease with Raphael and Adams and even Tarkington—then all the genuine art of the past does indeed begin to smack of intellectual elitism. And indeed, it wasn't long before the syndicated columnist Rod MacLeish began confessing that *he'd* always regarded Marcel Proust as "an impenetrable bore." By the same token, Hawthorne's *The Scarlet Letter* was "a drag," as we say in the literary community, and "a prissy piece of drivel" to boot. Vivaldi and Bret Harte were positively soporific ("if you've read one Harte story you've read 'em all"), Melville too was a bore, and so was just about everybody else who'd had the luck to walk the planet before Roderick MacLeish had arrived on the literary scene. "Honestly, now," tittered Mr. MacLeish, "have you gotten through *Moby Dick* more than once?"

By definition, of course, the MacLeishes of the world are incompatible with the Hawthornes and the Mel-villes and the Shakespeares of the world; but as the months wore on, the spirit of MacLeish seemed to be spreading with unusual speed. Peter Prescott of *News-week* took out after Carlyle and Tennyson and Kingsley (the hapless trio actually believed in "chivalric ideals," and "they really thought that the Arthurian legends

represented virtues still relevant to industrial England,"
the fools), and the *New York Review of Books* found
room in its pages for bitter attacks against the celebrated
classical scholars of the past ("Edwardian dons and
floggers" who believed in "an ancient world of their
own creation"). Even the great Edith Hamilton (whom
John Mason Brown had once described as "a citizen of
two worlds, the ancient and the modern, and equally at
home with the best of both") was a "Hellenophile,"
according to the *Review*, a purveyor of "antiseptic,
innocent fantasies dear to certain pedagogues." Certain
pedagogues at the *New York Review of Books* were big
boys who knew what Life was all about, bless their
sophisticated little hearts, and they weren't about to be
taken in by the illusion of glory or honor: after all, they
had all the anti-intellectual "weapons" of the modern
"classical armory" at their disposal (including "Marx
and Freud," of all people), and—like the other savagers
of the past—they were determined to use anything at
hand. Richard Corliss of *Time* magazine joined the
chorus, speaking for "modern readers" who couldn't
stomach the "stodgy virtues" of Charles Dickens' characters, characters who were "pasteboard clichés of
middle-class sentimentality," and even Graham Greene
found it necessary to begin a new book of essays by
noting that Thomas Carlyle was "a great Scottish
bore"—a notation that shed a lot more light on the
attention span of Graham Greene than it did on the
literary skill of Thomas Carlyle.

Some of the most embarrassing symptoms surfaced
down at the *Washington Post*, where a witty television
critic named Thomas Shales was taking time off from

his normal duties to stick out a less-than-witty tongue at Sir Walter Scott's "just-as-well-forgotten novel," *Ivanhoe*. Mr. Shales was really a rather superior sort of critic, and his offenses against his betters were mild compared to those committed by the *Post*'s house philosopher Richard Cohen, who was letting everybody know that although he'd dutifully read "the dirty parts," as he called them, of D.H. Lawrence and Henry Miller ("who, I reluctantly concluded after a lot of page turning, has a wholly undeserved reputation as a dirty writer"), he'd never been able to plough through boring stuff like *War and Peace, The Brothers Karamazov, Bleak House, Paradise Lost, Pride and Prejudice, Man's Fate*, Keats, Shelley, Wordsworth, Burke, Hardy, or "the Marshall McLuhan of his time," Aristotle ("I'm sure once he is understood, his reputation will suffer"). Why heck, confessed Mr. Cohen, he couldn't even handle *Tom Sawyer* or *Huckleberry Finn*, let alone *Moby Dick*: "I cannot read the book," said he with boyish pride.

A bewildered reading public naturally assumed that some kind of soul at the *Post* would take the boy aside and gently but firmly direct him to a new career, but those hopes were dashed a few days later when Mr. Cohen's assistant managing editor threw his own hat into the ring: "I confess to never having read F.A. Hayek's *Road to Serfdom*," thundered the editor, winning points for imagination. Being an editor at the *Washington Post*, he had to take the mandatory copulatory digression ("for the longest time in my burning adolescent years I actually thought 'laissez faire' was a dirty French expression for 'let's do it' "), but he finished up with a flourish: "When I was in college, I confess, I fell asleep over Locke and Mill and Adam Smith."

By this time, however, the competition to decide which writer couldn't read the most books was threatening to get out of hand, and there was a general sigh of relief when the publishing house of Harper and Row announced that it would no longer publish *any* books that could not first prove to a "marketing computer" that they would show "a substantial return." Henry James and Herman Melville be damned: in times of intellectual frenzy you don't take chances with the company product, Buster; and if even *War and Peace* was a bore, if *The Scarlet Letter* was a Prissy Piece of Drivel, what was a publisher to do?

The firm of Harper and Row was, in fact, one of the best of the lot (if only because it was one of the few that still had room for genuine editors, such as Aaron Asher, who could tell the difference between serious and frivolous writing, and who cared about the difference). But even well-intentioned firms were beginning to buckle under pressure from the competition. The pressure itself was social and economic in nature, but the spirit it fed on was the spirit of collective guilt, the guilt of a literary generation that had failed and shamed its ancestors, and knew it.

It hadn't felt like guilt at first; it had felt like irreverence, or sophistication. It was an attitude that had been born in the epigrammatic chatter of fashionable drawing rooms in the 1880s, encouraged by the celebration of animality that followed the first World War, and maintained by the institutionalized self-hatred that was part of the legacy of the second (and the smell of the third). What had begun as the insolent exhibitionism of an Oscar Wilde had ended as the ugly hatred of a warped child for its parents' happiness.

Some of those who might have been expected to say a good word for the past helped to savage it instead, without really understanding what they were doing. Within a few years of the end of the second World War, even the good fellow Edward Weeks was reminiscing in public about an editorial meeting that had been called at the offices of the *Atlantic Monthly* to consider "the merits of an overly nice biographical portrait of John Ruskin"; and speaking with evident approval of a fellow editor who had expressed a desire to give Ruskin "a good kick in the pants."

It had seemed funny at the time; but even then, there had been something unpleasant beneath the schoolboy giggles. The question inevitably arose: Why? Why did Edward Weeks like the idea of ridiculing John Ruskin? After all, Mr. Weeks was not a Philistine; on the contrary, he was something of a nobleman—personally, editorially, and intellectually. Did Ruskin offend by his goodness? By his earnestness? By his generosity? Not really. No, John Ruskin was a thorn in the editorial side because he was—John Ruskin. The memory of his greatness constituted a silent reproach; and he was resented for that reason. Irreverence was not really irreverence at all: it was shame. Not the personal shame of an Edward Weeks, whose intentions were (and are) always honorable; but the intellectual and spiritual shame of an entire culture.

In publishing circles, the guilt became an industry of

bitterness: the late 1970s and early 1980s saw the publication of a series of revelatory biographies that sought to strip the nobility from men like Housman, Kingsley, Gladstone, T.E. Lawrence, Arnold, and even Ruskin, to render great souls comprehensible (and less threatening) to smaller souls. It was Stracheyism without wit or integrity, savagery with no purpose but the destruction of high aspiration and the exaltation of the animalism that may be found even in angels. Some of the books and articles were better than others, and some of the biographers genuinely admired, or thought they admired, their victims; but all of them—consciously or unconsciously—sought to define greatness in terms of its flaws, rather than the other way around. It was an unholy union of the three virulent fevers that had haunted the democratic centuries at every step of the way: envy and greed and despair.

One publishing house—St. Martin's Press—seemed to symbolize the entire reactionary movement when it showed up on Grub Street with an erotic homosexual version of the biblical Books of Samuel. The gospel according to St. Martin's was from the hand of the author of *Christopher and Gay* and *Coming Out*, and it Came Out something like this:

> David stiffened his body. "Saul! No!"
> "What do you mean, 'no'?" Saul's eyes blazed.
> "Not like this!"
> "Like what I say! Roll over, boy, and spread that pretty rump."
> David was rigid. "No!"

And this:

> Arad pulled his tunic over his head and dropped it

to the floor of the tent.... The half-globes of his buttocks seemed opulent on his lean frame, firm with the tension of the cold, and smooth as a girl's. Saul, David thought with satisfaction, would be cared for. He reached over and took a cruet of fragrant oil, pouring some of it in his hand. "Bend over and spread your..."

But enough is enough. (Or, as St. Martin's Arad remarks, when King David's "oily fingers" investigate a particularly delicate "crevice": "Ow!") The blurb writers at St. Martin's Press said it well: "The ringing names of the Old Testament become hungry, fallible human beings, burning with life." A headline writer at the *Washington Star* said it better, as he addressed himself to a new biography of Matthew Arnold: "Down From the Pedestal."

If the pedestal-smashers had an argument, it was the one advanced by E.M. Forster in his 1939 essay, "What I Believe":

> Hero-worship is a dangerous vice, and one of the minor merits of a democracy is that it does not encourage it, or produce that unmanageable type of citizen known as the Great Man. It produces instead different kinds of small men—a much finer achievement.... No, I distrust Great Men. They produce a desert of uniformity around them and often a pool of blood too, and I always feel a little man's pleasure when they come a cropper.

Just so. Mr. Forster was not a Philistine, but he was a stunted man, spiritually, emotionally, and professionally. He was one of those sad creatures of the twentieth century who define themselves in terms of their own insufficiencies, and it was his tragedy—and ours, some may think—that he let his unhappiness and his self-reproach lead him to bitterness and weakness, rather to greatness and strength. The key phrase in his chilling celebration of envy is the one about great men being "unmanageable." They are, of course. But the perverted social democracy that would deprive itself of great souls in order that smaller souls might strut is a democracy that would banish splendor from the earth on the grounds that the warmth from that splendor cannot be felt by all. It is a gospel of death.

The novelist Mary Renault recently traced the true outline of the snake beneath the glib justifications:

> There are always men who take their own measure against greatness, and hate it not for what it is, but for what they are. They can envy even the dead.

And the novelist identified the poison as well, the poison that has, in one form or another, helped to dissolve every social contract in history. It was, she said,

> the power such men have to rouse in others the sleeping envy they once had a decent shame of; to turn respect for excellence into hate.

Chapter XI

Redefining Art

In time, those members of the community who were farthest away from the emergency exits began bashing madly away at the immutable boundaries of art and philosophy, on the old theory that if everything was art, then nothing was art—and you couldn't be prosecuted for intellectual crimes against something that had never existed in the first place, could you?

It was in such a spirit of false ecumenicity that the ordinarily sensible editors of the *New Republic* resolved to turn over large chunks of their "Books and the Arts" department to a pack of garrulous punk-rock fans. The New Wave Republicans were soon torturing their dazed subscribers with interminable analyses of things like Professor Longhair's *Crawfish Fiesta* (the professor's "last and best album"), *The Wall* ("never less than titillating"), *Get Happy* ("ferocious intensity"), and *The Pretenders* ("an extraordinary debut" by a band of "new wave neoclassicists").

And yet, even as they rocked, the kids seemed to sense that there was something a bit odd about their new responsibilities: "It has become obvious," said rock-Republican Jim Miller, "that many of the most interesting developments in rock are no longer likely to reach many people." He knew something was happening, but he didn't know what it was: "The implications are not yet clear," confessed Mr. Miller, who just couldn't dig why so many of his fellow intellectuals weren't Being Reached by "albums that challenge received ideas about the links between rock and roll and popular culture." The poor chap might just as well have been musing about the Received Ideas of Joyce Carol Oates or Barbara Cartland: the jargon of literary criticism had become interchangeable with the patter of Punk Rock, and—this was the interesting factor—nobody noticed. The actual object of criticism—the work under discussion—had become a complete irrelevancy. It was not even essential that there *be* a subject. What mattered was that the critical chatter itself should endure, week after week, month after month, decade after decade, all the buzzing phrases in all the proper places. Elvis Costello, John Updike, *Sophie's Choice* or *Crawfish Fiesta*, it was all one and the same to the remnants of the professional literary community: the criticism had assumed a life of its own in a world of its own, and anything was fair game.

And Jim Miller of the *New Republic* could buzz along with the best of them: "For ten minutes the song circles methodically around the unpromising line 'I know you very well/You are unbearable.' Squealing and jabbering and moaning at the top of his range, [the singer] sounds like a man turned inside out." Therefore: "There is something oddly compelling about this album. Since I first heard it, I've scarcely stopped playing it, perhaps because the music manages to be simultaneously erotic and repulsive." It was no wonder that the *New Republic* saw itself appealing to a "college-educated audience": nobody else would have stood for the bluff. Presumably those who did stand for it were the sort of college-educated folk who liked "Books and Arts" by rock singers who rummaged through "the trash bins of urban life, collecting stereotypes and truisms, scrambling them out of order and then welding them back into a collage that jars our expectations," and all that sort of thing. What the star-struck Mr. Miller admired most of all was "the very bluntness" with which his favorite Artists "confronted the listener," not to mention that good old "needling sense of passion, however inchoate or unattractive some of the sentiments may be." And please God, it was all so terribly terribly important: "There has never been anything quite like it before in rock and roll," and hey, "the boundaries of rock are being redrawn," and don't you kids out there *care* anymore?

The *New Republic* didn't dance to the music for very long (the magazine was one of the most serious in the country, and its editors knew when to pull back from an abyss), but the indefatigable Mr. Miller kept right on moving to the beat of his superannuated drummer, and soon he could be found in the sleaziest of rock and roll heavens (*Newsweek* magazine), buzzing happily about some poor "prophet of sexual anarchy" who preached "salvation through sexuality," or something (we don't *explain* this stuff, we just report it), by means of a "blunt album of hard-core lyrics about lust, loss and the freedom to do anything you want—from dodging the draft to sleeping with your sister." "He's got a skimpy mustache, a wild shock of hair and eyes that flash fire," gushed the literary bobbysoxer; my dears, he was "such a fascinating figure," you wouldn't believe it. Dear old *Newsweek*.

The Prophet of Sexual Anarchy's "appetite for sex developed...when he found a cache of pornography hidden in his mother's bedroom," and Mr. Miller could only thank the gods for such favors. The critic was particularly taken with a poster of his hero "half naked and dripping wet, posed next to a small crucifix," but he was also pretty keen on the "nearly nude picture on the album cover," and on an accompanist who "writhed around her keyboard in skimpy underwear and rain-coat." It was all so...so *artistic*. Like Paris in the Twenties, like Berlin in the Thirties, like Frisco in the Sixties. And as for the music itself: well, "Dirty Mind" had been great, just great, but "Sexuality," "Do Me Baby," and "I Wanna Be Your Lover" were just, well, Wow, you know? We mean, "there's simply no one better."

Mr. Miller had just been to see his hero in person, and he was still trembling. Why, the whole Experience had been "a razzle-dazzle riot of erotic funk," squealed the critic, his excitement mounting: "He pantomimes making love...He bumps, he grinds, he does a strip-tease...he caresses every word, pleads, preens, rears back, and screams. He holds the moment captive—and gives us a glimpse of one man's ecstasy." Well we *bet* he did, Jim. "In an era of conservative chic the words needle, taunt and make brilliant theatrical sense," gasped the exhausted little fan at one point, wiping the sweat from his brow.

Ah yes, the words. And what *were* the words? Well:

> People call me rude
> I wish we all were nude
> I wish there was no black or white
> I wish there were no rules.

One more time: "I wish there were no rules." That's what the *Chicago Tribune*'s cultural affairs correspondent was trying to say when he adopted Mr. Miller's cast-off Sexual Prophet (who was "challenging" all the scariest "stereotypes of today," according to the *Tribune*'s boy), and that's what the class cutups at *Newsweek* were trying to say when they moved Mr. Miller over to the book department: We wish there were no rules. If there was anything interesting about the hoary old chant, it was that it should have reappeared so late in the human game, just as the lights seemed to be going out. It was something almost dead, something left over from prehistoric times: it was the penultimate chorus of the Everlasting Whimper, and it was being chanted by the bored and overeducated children of the most affluent and literate and tawdry civilization in history.

But there *were* rules. Even Jim Miller knew that. The proof of his secret concession was to be detected in the slightly hysterical tone of his writings: a critic who really has something to say about art does not need to spend his time trying to persuade his readers that he is in fact writing about art. Just as the antics of an unruly tot often constitute a plea for attention, so did Mr. Miller's immature sexual meditations constitute a plea to be taken seriously. The condition was a temporary one, presumably: children do grow up, and Mr. Miller would eventually come to understand what so many of his predecessors had come to understand (often to their everlasting sorrow)—that a writer begins to be taken seriously by serious people only when and if he or she begins to speak of serious things.

There are not many rules, for art or for life; but those that do exist are simple, eternal, unalterable, and—most important—universally understood, even by those who struggle against them. As Sir Thomas Browne put it, more than three centuries ago:

> Live by old Ethicks and the classical Rules of Honesty. Put no new names or notions upon Authentic Virtues and Vices. Think not that Morality is Ambulatory; that Vices in one Age are not Vices in another; or that Virtues, which are under the everlasting Seal of right Reason, may be Stamped by Opinion. And therefore, though vicious times invert the opinions of things, and set up new Ethicks against Virtue, yet hold thou unto old Morality; and rather than follow a multitude to do evil, stand like Pompey's Pillar conspicuous by thyself, and single in Integrity.

Those who were "single in Integrity" did exist, of course, even in 1980; and they were not so isolated as they felt themselves to be.

> And since the worst of times afford imitable Examples of Virtue; since no Deluge of Vice is like

to be so general, but more than eight will escape;
Eye well those Heroes who have held their Heads
Above Water, who have touched Pitch, and not
been defiled, and in the common Contagion have
remained uncorrupted.

Just as there are heroes in every disaster, so were there
individual writers and periodicals and professors and
critics who sought to keep their heads above the increasingly fetid literary oceans, and so were there editors and
publishers who sought to give them a hand. Honest
men and women at Harcourt Brace Jovanovich, Harper
and Row, Ticknor and Fields, W.W. Norton, Van-
guard, many of the university presses, Farrar Straus and
Giroux, Houghton Mifflin, Holt Rinehart and Win-
ston, and some four or five other large houses were still
trying to hold the line against increasing pressure from
Dutton, Times Books, Delacorte, and all the other giant
merchants of computerized sleaze. These few well-
intentioned editors and executives were supported in
their thankless efforts by dozens of smaller independent
publishers scattered about the North American continent and the United Kingdom, most of whom could not
discover their potential audience—the quiet readers
who still cared for real books and real ideas—because
that audience had no way of finding out about them or
their publications.

It was true that even the least responsible firms still
published a few serious books (if only because the
members of the boards of directors had to have *something* to put on their coffee tables), but it was also true
that even the most responsible houses were being forced
to issue more and more bad books (few serious books

were reviewed by popular critics), and that the bad books were getting worse. And there was a new phenomenon as well, a phenomenon unprecedented (as we said in those days) in the short history of American publishing: the existence of a few large hardcover publishing houses—no more than three or four—that had abandoned all sham, and no longer even pretended to have anything to do with literature.

Chief among the mutants was the giant house of E.P. Dutton (now Elsevior-Dutton), which was advertising one of its new volumes as "a sadomasochistic experience of frightening intensity" ("so extreme in its sexuality that it takes the reader's breath away"), another as "a psychosexual guide to ourselves via our footwear" (it included a long peek at, God help us, "the most pornographic shoe ever worn"), another as "a revolutionary guide to sexual acupuncture" (no questions please), and a fourth as "a.valuable catalog" of "the most important problem of our relations and attitudes to excrement" (the awful object was called *End Product*). For the higher-class sort of reader Dutton was stocking things like *The Star Trek Reader* and *The World According to Garp*—which is to say that Dutton no longer had the slightest interest in readers of the higher classes. Only a few worthy survivors of a better time— B.J. Chute, Wilfrid Sheed, Borges, the Dent reprints— remained as ghostly reminders of what the firm had once represented. By 1980, a once-proud publishing house had become the embarrassment of the trade, and—this is the point—no one seemed to care.

It is true that the rapid destruction of Dutton's reputation during the late 1970s was almost entirely the work of one editor (who shall remain nameless, because recently deceased), but perhaps that is the real lesson: twenty good men or women occupying positions of authority in a cultural democracy can give a nation a civilized literature, if not a great one; twenty irresponsible men or women occupying the same places can shame an entire people.

At The Cinema

The awful howls of diminishing influence grew ever louder, and finally even the *New York Review of Books*, which had been expected to review the books of New York until the bitter end, suddenly jumped ship and came floating rather groggily to the surface with a series of articles about old movie comedians and folk singers. Caught by surprise, the *Washington Post*'s *Book World* slapped a sketch of the comic Woody Allen onto its own cover and paid a Distinguished Professor of Renaissance Literature (Samuel Schoenbaum of the University of Maryland) to come up with an essay about Mr. Allen's new "collection of comic writing." "A wonderfully gifted creative presence," sighed the professor happily, and nobody had the decency to tell the poor chap that the Wonderful Presence had only written another volume of funny stories. In the Panic of 1980, it was every man for himself; and the distinguished professor went on to prove it by scurrying up to Boston to take part in the obscenity trial of the film *Caligula*, which—as every student of *very* early Renaissance Literature must now know—was produced by the hipsters from *Penthouse* as a guide to "various forms of sexual practice and torture in the first century."

Professor Schoenbaum was very much a man of the world, of course, and he wasn't much bothered by any of that old "sexual practice" stuff, not even, as he said later, all that "oral sex, complete to the final spasm"; but he did suggest rather shamefacedly that he'd been just a *leetle* bit upset by a few of the more "hideously drawn out" torture scenes. Still, unlike the rest of us in those dark times, this particular man of the world took, Ahem, "a very serious view of the Constitution and the rights guaranteed by the First Amendment," so he did his intellectual duty, right up there on the witness stand: he looked that old judge straight in the eye and told him that the movie had "serious artistic value," because it had John Gielgud and Peter O'Toole in it, and hadn't Peter O'Toole been nominated for an Oscar *five times*? Well, there you were, your Honor, there you were. Informed sources had to admit that not even *Saturday Night Fever* had received so many important nominations. And anyway, continued Professor Schoenbaum, he seemed to remember having read somewhere that the Emperor Caligula had presided over "an orgiastic court unfettered by moral constraints," and somehow it followed that movie theaters in Boston ought to be at least as unfettered as the Court of Caligula. After all, this was America, and it was the twentieth century, and that kind of thing.

The Distinguished Professor of Renaissance Literature wasn't a DPRL for nothing: as a matter of fact, he was the only man in the game who could say with authority that the *Penthouse* script had more "historic-

ity" than one of Shakespeare's lesser-known plays, and
he said it, and, well, it just about stopped the show dead.
But not for long: the nervous academic was joined in
the cultural chorus line by a rather specialized person
from California who had devoted her life to the study of
the mechanical aspects of the rarest varieties of human
sexual activity. This person had flown all the way
across the country in order to tell the people of Massachusetts that certain explicit sexual scenes in *Caligula*
had "educational" value. She didn't explain why on
earth the people of Massachusetts or any other state
ought to be at all interested in her opinions about
anything, and after a few minutes she went away again.
Still, it had been an inspiring sight, this chance con-
junction of sexology and historicity, and it gave the
cultural and academic communities a brief moment of
false hope: perhaps art *could* be redefined, or even
liquidated; perhaps Ultimate Meanings *could* be measured in terms of Oscar nominations and final spasms!

It was a time of delightful madness, and it lasted for
just a few more minutes, as the stand was taken by a
slightly less Distinguished but no less determined professor from Harvard. His name was Bowersock, he said:
he was the head of the classics department, and of course
he had also been a consultant at the National Endowment for the Humanities. Professor Bowersock implied
that the Art in question wasn't quite kinky enough:
there were, it seemed, "even more revolting episodes in
the ancient sources." For reasons which he neglected to
divulge, the classicist wanted Americans to "contemplate the facts that one would rather not contemplate,"
though he stopped short of insisting that matinée per-

formances of *Caligula* be made mandatory in the nation's universities. Unfortunately, other folks had apparently stopped short of insisting that certain books by Stobart, Scullard, and some twenty other authorities be made mandatory reading in Harvard's classics department: "For me, this has drawn attention to the neglect of a formative period in the early Roman empire," revealed the professor, who imagined, somewhat surprisingly, that Caligula's reign had been "ignored until recent times." "History can be very unpleasant," he concluded darkly, drawing on his vast store of arcane knowledge.

But if history could be unpleasant, the study of history could be rather a kick in the head: under questioning, the witness shed a bit of light on the state of his own art by explaining that he'd accepted a $2,000 check from *Penthouse*, proving once again that underneath all that tinsel and glamour, Hollywood literati were Just Like Folks. (It was all horribly proper, of course: it is customary for "expert witnesses" to receive a fee for their time and testimony, and American academics are nothing if not customary. The shame came not from the money, but from its source.) And on this magic night in the history of the cinema, Professor Bowersock had some good news and some bad news: he was leaving Harvard, he said, and going to Princeton. In the emotional aftermath of the announcement, all agreed that it had been a truly marvelous episode in the Redefinition of Art, perhaps the last of its kind, and a real slap in the face for the enemy (if indeed there was an enemy). But in the cold light of dawn, the awful fear returned, and it was even stronger than before: "Nobody asked me if I enjoyed *Caligula*," muttered Professor Schoenbaum of Maryland somewhat defensively, implying that he'd really put one over on judge, jury, and nation, if not on himself. But then, perhaps he was just beginning to realize that he'd miscalculated the going rate for expert artistic sensibility: "I had asked for $1,000," said the Distinguished Professor of Renaissance Literature, "and in the end a check for a thou awaited me in Boston." The silver screen had claimed its latest victim, and another cultural escape hatch had been slammed shut.

The former "*Penthouse* Pet of the Year" who played Messalina in the film had the final artistic word on the whole debacle. "Those sexual scenes are the *hardest* to do," she said. "One scene, we shot for two days: one scene, two days. It was exhausting."

Meanwhile, back at the *Washington Post*, the terrified monks were devoting considerable attention to a book called *The Durable Fig Leaf*, which was, sad to say, *A Historical, Cultural, Medical, Social, Literary, and Iconographic Account of Man's Relations With His Penis*. "The last decade has already seen a number of important books on this subject," said the *Post*'s reviewer, presumably with a scholarly frown; nevertheless, *Fig Leaf* made "a legitimate point," which was that "since prehistoric times, man has been preoccupied with his"—well, with his, you know. (The *Post* didn't say just which man had been so preoccupied, but the guessing around town was that he probably worked for a Major National Newspaper.) In any case, by the time the literary gang at the *Post* got around to recommending *Breasts: Women Speak About Their Breasts and Their Lives,* all caution had been thrown to the winds. The book was, by golly, "an important contribution," and it packed an unusual message as well: "The message of this book is for women to make friends with their breasts," gulped the *Post*'s reviewer, no doubt suppressing a sentimental sob or two. The illustrations were particularly impressive, to a bookish mind: "As the photographs demonstrate, breasts come in tremendous variety." Ivory-tower types might have been stunned to learn that "there are big breasts and little breasts," but that was the kind of year it was, a year of intellectual ferment. "My only criticism," concluded the worried critic, "is that so few of the women interviewed seemed to have a sense of humor about their breasts." It was the judgment of the *Post* that "a lighter touch might help women feel better about their breasts—and themselves."

But by that time, of course, the situation had degenerated far beyond the point at which a healthy giggle or two might have done some good: just as all living men and women had become great artists, so had everything that issued from those men and women become "art," or "literature," or "thought"; and the guardians of the universal gallery had long ago misplaced the only rule book that could have told them how to tell the difference between a giggle and a masterpiece.

The general inability to distinguish between the true and the false was a consequence of the calculated destruction of all established principle and purpose. How is it possible to be genuinely serious—about art or literature or humanity—if one does not know *why* one is supposed to be serious, or just what it is that one is supposed to be serious about? How is it possible for a child to assume the aspect of an adult, if the child does not yet understand the language of maturity? It is not possible; and the effort to seem without being always leads to farce.

But it *is* possible for a child to dress up in the clothes of an adult, and for him to persuade *other* children that he has assumed the aspect of maturity. The college freshman with his first pipe or the fifteen-year-old with a hint of a mustache may make his elders smile, but he succeeds in his primary aim, which is to persuade his own friends (and himself) that he is something more than a child. Those who are not yet formed—who have as yet no purpose or principle to guide their thought or their behavior or their writing—invariably define themselves in terms of the opinion and the conduct of others. Such people live for the favor of their peers: they stand ready to adopt any view or sentiment, or pursue any course of conduct, provided only that it be popular, or at least sanctioned, in immediate circles. If other popular magazines are printing hymns of praise to "erotic and repulsive" recordings, shouldn't our magazine be doing the same? If a Major Publisher has seen fit to publish an expensive analysis of human excrement, aren't we obligated to look at it, to take it seriously, to review it? If people are tolerating John Updike or standing in line to see pornographic movies, doesn't that mean that John Updike and pornographic movies are...are okay? Surely the other magazines can't be *wrong*, surely a Major Publisher can't be an *idiot*, surely people can't be *bad*? There is no *bad*, is there? It's all *good*, isn't it? It *must* be good, because others are doing it.

It is not hard to see how such an attitude of intellectual subservience leads to perpetual anxiety, and eventually to real mental panic. A now-forgotten (and never very famous) clergyman from Connecticut named Joel Hawes described the process, "on the twenty-seventh day of April, in the fifty-third year of Independence of the United States of America":

> It is always easy to know what is right; but often very difficult to know what is for our present interest or popularity. The man who acts from false principles is often thrown into great straits. He knows not what course to pursue, or how to avoid the difficulties that are ever thickening around him. His way is dark and crooked; and full of snares and pits. He lives in a state of constant suspicion and fear. A dreadful sound is in his ears; he trembles at the rustling of a leaf, and is compelled to have recourse to various dishonest acts and shifts to avoid detection and punishment.

In the early years of the third century "of Independence of the United States of America," personal independence—of intellect or character or action—was in extremely short supply, because purpose and integrity and understanding were in short supply; and many of the nation's wealthiest and most educated citizens lived from deadline to deadline with a dreadful sound in their ears, and trembled at the rustling of a leaf.

Chapter XII

The Important Subject

Sex is so very important; it is probably the most
important thing. What is more important? I know
of nothing.

Gay Talese

It was often said, with some truth, that the magazines
and newspapers that carried and celebrated the deadly
literary fevers were merely the most noticeable victims
of the spreading intellectual hysteria, hapless recipients
of the general despair. It might also have been said, with
at least as much truth, that the artistic madness was
itself merely the most pretentious and vicious manifestation of a common and incessant journalistic frenzy.
But then, it was a distinguishing feature of the cultural
democracy that it tended to blur and finally corrupt the
ancient and useful distinctions—to confuse literature
with journalism, art with decoration, the host with the
parasite. In the late 1970s and early 1980s, English and

American journalists—the police reporters and the political analysts and the gossip columnists and the local commentators—operated within the same neighborhoods (and in many cases were the same people) as the novelists and the poets and the editors and the critics. Casual reportorial mood, good or bad, could—and usually did—quickly become deep artistic and intellectual ritual; and we cannot begin to appreciate the virulence of the cultural disease until we identify the peculiar anguish of the young journalists who suffered from its effects and transmitted its germ.

Microcosm On The Potomac

And what an unusually single-minded anguish it was, in its journalistic form: the anguish of a nervous intellectual imposter who is determined to keep the conversation hovering around one minor observation because he knows he would have little to say about any of the major implications.

Inevitably, the *Washington Post* was a characteristic case in point. The same reform-minded editors who had once chattered dizzily about giving the *Wall Street Journal* some real competition as a national newspaper now found themselves proofing long stories about suburban "erotica parties" and making room on the front page for things like "The Boy-Whore World." As the largest newspaper in the nation's capital grew increasingly shrill in its challenge to the *National Enquirer*, the headlines turned giggly ("Honk if You're Celibate," "Gay Couples Living Together," "Strip Suits,"

"When I Take Off My Dress and Start Singing") the writing grew gigglier ("hot tubs, computer dating, post-coital cigarettes and Frederick's of Hollywood"), and the editorial section positively freaked out: "Nude Dancing, Without Guilt." There were suspiciously heated attacks against uncooperative persons who were "unhappy in their smug, self-righteous defense of asexuality," there was a sudden glut of bizarre "medical" articles ("Drugs and Sex," "Sex Among the Mentally Ill"), and there were weird guides to the national political conventions: "If you left the someone you usually fondle back home, it's up to you to opt or not for a temporary sub. However you ought to know that there are more than twenty infections (not to mention other kinds of things that are joked about but not spoken of) which can be affectionately transmitted." There was a senior staff writer who panned a new film because it was "hardly more erotic than an early-morning visit to the Eastern Market." (all his "hopes of competent pornography" had "been dashed"), and, inevitably, there were sex guides ("Sex After Sixty," "What Makes A Man Good In Bed") and more sex guides: "These days, in the thick layer of Washington that's young and citified, it's generally considered okay if you sleep with somebody on the first date."

That "young and citified thick layer," of course, was one of the literary establishment's wistful little euphemisms for "some of the kids here at the office," and its appearance in the middle of a guide to sexual promiscuity was more than a little revealing, if only because it implied the extent to which the Layer was out of touch—socially, morally, and intellectually—with the people it wished to impress and represent. For decades the popular intelligentsia of the middle-brow had, in Pamela Hansford Johnson's phrase, "clung to the petticoats of fashion with the frenzy of an infant terrified to be parted from its mother," and now the petticoats were being pulled away, and the kids knew it, and they were scared. Sweatier and sweatier they grew, winding themselves up tighter and tighter in the one soiled petticoat that still seemed to be attached to the sales figures, until finally all the world had become one giant erotic maze: "Do you hold off until the next date or even the next month?" (What *do* you do, out there in the real world, up above the Layer? What are you thinking about?) And always, lurking just beneath the surface of the protracted snicker, there was the secret fear that some of the younger observers on the scene, like the older ones who mattered, might no longer be paying much attention to the psychological confusions of one thin generation of troubled journalists and critics. There were, in one *Post* writer's inadvertent metaphor for the larger condition, "vast numbers of people out there who find this first-date intimacy upsetting." And God help us, they *were* "out there," those vast numbers, out there in the Real World, and they were getting closer and they were oh so horribly different from you and me: "For them, there is the second date."

That random remark, like so many others, defined the spiritual and intellectual boundaries within which the Community's daily commentators had dropped their philosophical petticoats, and for months to come the journalistic air was musty with the odor of unwashed linen.

Seized with literary ambition, some of the more businesslike reporters at the paper in question began competing with one another to see who could come up with the sleaziest sexual memoir ("the fear we've fought and the lovers we've left"). One young woman offered an anecdote about an "ex-lover" who had "moved out" on her after a battle over his sleeping habits, a male colleague contributed a criticism of a former wife who kept interrupting him at Awkward Moments during his career as a "Recent Single" ("Let me, uh, just put my shoes on"), and an even sadder young female reporter seemed to speak for the whole group of exiles when she said:

> Everybody is somebody's ex-lover.... June broke up with the best friend and started living with Tim. Bill and I lived together. June and Tim lived across the street. Jack and Jill were our friends.... Bill and I broke up. I moved to a friend's house for a while. Bill started dating her. She was also dating....

At that point in her reminiscences the child began to get a little confused, but the gist of her life—and her spirit—was clear. And no, these "reporters" were not shown the door. On the contrary, they were encouraged—nay, required—to pursue their peculiar activities in the interests of the public's right to know (which had long ago superseded the public's right not to give a damn).

As always, the *Post*'s resident pundit, Richard Cohen, managed to stay just one grunt ahead of his younger colleagues. On some mornings Mr. Cohen could be found delivering monologues about his young "manhood," when he was "no longer either a teen-ager or chaste": "Time took care of the former and a girl named Leonore took care of the latter sometime in my 19th year." On other days he could be found reminiscing about his more recent studies: "It is hard to believe that...there is not, from time to time, just a little bit of sex going on outside the home. Speaking personally, it was years before I considered a car primarily as a means of transportation." And on every other day he could be seen underfoot, muttering about his current confusions: "It takes a real man to admit he's unmanly.... There are lots of men who would prefer to be something other than the stereotypical male.... Some of them would rather that the women in their lives initiated the dates, or at least some of them, and shared the expense of them and maybe—just maybe—initiated the sex also."

Did anybody read the awful stuff? Apparently not. But that didn't really matter to its authors. Their incessant sexual musings constituted a form of therapy, a way of dealing with unhappiness and resentment. And indeed, it was the resentment—the everlasting whine—that came through most clearly. For reasons best left unexplored, Mr. Cohen shared with his colleagues a deep-seated dislike for anything that smacked of light or youth or health or purity; and, like his colleagues, he nursed the forlorn hope that he might negate normal life by smearing it with his own suffocating preoccupations. He was, in other words, the sort of person who could and did sneer at a young girl in the public eye because she seemed to him "to be a virgin": "Such things are rare," hissed Mr. Cohen, who moved in very limited circles. In Cohen circles, young people who were not promiscuous were "rare birds, who lack, at the very least, a certain zest for experimentation," and their frightening restraint was "contrary to the very nature of youth." Such people seemed to threaten Mr. Cohen in some way. Their sweetness seemed to imply the existence of some huge and different world "out there," a world that Mr. Cohen would never visit or comprehend. He hated it.

More often, though, the literary spit was directed not at some luckless individual but at a whole generation:

> There is some feeling that to be a chaste teen-ager is a wonderful thing. Why that is, I do not know. I do know that as a chaste teen-ager, you spend much of your time attempting to remedy this situation. This means that you do not do your schoolwork or anything else that will interfere with your single-minded attempt to get unchaste as soon as possible. Chaste teen-agers are always thinking of chastity, unchastity and allied subjects.

But of course by this time the *Washington Post*'s readers had a pretty good idea of just who it was who was "always thinking of chastity, unchastity and allied subjects."

It has been said that it is only the very middle-aged who imagine that the young spend most of their lives hopping in and out of bed with no talk or thought of love or fidelity. The statement is true as far as it goes (which is to say that few genuine youths would have been able to recognize themselves or their generation in Mr. Cohen's unsavory ramblings). But the peculiar vision of youth as a perpetual orgy—which would be laughable if it were not so unutterably pitiful—is not a fantasy of premature middle age, but of emotional insufficiency. Only the deficient and inexperienced soul can really believe that fundamental human emotions can change from century to century; only the shallow heart seeks to soothe itself by telling itself that all hearts are shallow.

Like most genuinely sad spectacles, the insistent exhibitionism eventually became a bit of a farce. In later years, aficionados of rapid cultural decline would recall with a grimace the day the designers of the paper's Sunday op-ed pages threw out the egghead stuff in order to make room for a sexual lament that had originally appeared in the pages of—wait for it—the British *Cosmopolitan* magazine. The confession piece was signed by a Russian defector, and the subheadline said it all: "Prudishness, male chauvinist piggery and shortages make it tough to be a woman."

The *Post*'s borrowed foreign-affairs expert had one question, and only one question: "Do Russian women enjoy sex?" Well, "Soviet censorship" was "positively Victorian" (and what could be worse than that?), but Informed Sources had reason to believe that Russian men were "not very good lovers." Not only were they "prudes in their approach to lovemaking" (why, it was "considered indecent to see each other naked or to have a light on during intercourse"), but "lovemaking" was "not the first priority in a man's life"! Did you *ever*? Fortunately, there was "a booming black market in pornography" (defined by the author as "Western books and magazines"), to wit:

> People who can read foreign languages and have
> foreign connections get all the hot stuff: I read

The Story of O, Emmanuelle, Myra Breckenridge,
and issues of *Playboy* long before I defected....
Instead of selling books my friends and I used to
exchange them between ourselves.... I don't think
Solzhenitzen, who is austere and pious, would be
very happy if he knew that we used to exchange a
volume of the *Gulag*...in return for something by
Henry Miller—I loved *The Tropic of Cancer*—or
works by Harold Robbins, whom I wasn't so keen
on.

Clearly there was a place for this girl in American
journalism. She had all the jargon down pat, even the
bit about "the widespread notion that sexual attraction
is dirty and disgusting." She had all the proper con-
tacts: "I had one friend who told me she had had ten
abortions, and another boasted of six." She had the
essential editorial concerns: "The trouble is that con-
traceptives are poorly made and hard to come by. Men's
sheaths tend to be made of leaky plastic." She had the
requisite envy of people in high places: "There is a
small, privileged elite which can permit itself *la dolce
vita*.... These people indulge in all the perversions they
read about in Western publications, including 'group
sex.' I never saw any of this, of course, but a party of this
kind was once graphically described to us by one young
man at the institute who had just come back from one."
And finally she Viewed With Alarm the absence of
eroticism—"I see no signs of any refinement of tastes or
improvement in the behavior and attitudes"—while
embracing her new freedom: "I am happy to be out of
it."

Alas, the planners of the *Washington Post*'s Sunday
editorial sections were even happier to be Out Of It, and

they decided to express their democratic delirium by publishing a long political article written by—we swear it—a cartoonist from the *Village Voice*. The guy's name was Jules Feiffer (he was something of an icon, in predictable circles), and his article was "taken" from a speech he had made at the Washington School of the Institute for Policy Studies (in those days, no one wondered why cartoonists from the *Village Voice* were delivering lectures at the Institute for Policy Studies). It was Mr. Feiffer's thesis that good politicians were politicians with "sexual energy." For instance, Mr. Feiffer was not attracted by Jimmy Carter because Mr. Carter had "falsified sexual content to reach office." Franklin Roosevelt, on the other hand, "was nothing but sexual energy." "He was strong, he was vital, he was attractive...and in a wheelchair. Perfect! Safe sexual energy." Mr. Feiffer's view of life was, of course, precisely the view of life held by those who have wasted too many hours of their own lives gazing at sexy flicks in suburban movie theaters, and it was no surprise to learn that the hunky Mr. Roosevelt was just "like Jon Voight in *Coming Home*" (and you know how cool *Jon* was). It was Mr. Feiffer's long-held conviction that the Second World War would have been lost "if FDR were not sexy."

Unfortunately, Mr. Roosevelt's successor "lacked sex," and therefore "had to resort to A-bombs." Mr. Eisenhower radiated a "post-coital glow," and Lyndon Johnson really turned Mr. Feiffer on: "Raw, unharnessed sexual energy. It was as if Vietnam was a venereal by-product of LBJ's sexual drive, banging away to keep his dominoes up." The horrid little cartoonist's softporn approach to American history concluded, inevitably, with Mr. Feiffer's least favorite president, who was "pure porno—shady, sneaky, unkempt, skulking"—but enough.

It was hard enough to believe that the sad "satire" had been composed by a gainfully employed citizen who was well over the age of discretion (in fact he was, like so many of his rivals, just fifty years old, the father of a teen-aged daughter); but it was even harder to believe that the little chap's solitary ramblings had constituted part of a "lecture series" at the Washington School of the Institute for Policy Studies, and that the "lecture" had been attended by grown men and women, some of whom were graduates of secondary schools and even, we must presume, college. And it was almost impossible to believe that the words were actually being reprinted—deliberately and with premeditation—in the editorial section of a Major American Newspaper. Was it merely misguided satire? Therapy? A huge mistake?

We cannot really grasp the essential motivation behind the dissemination of hard-core trash until we have the courage to be rude, and to concede that the purveyors of such unattractive fare are often pretty unattractive themselves. Sometimes, as in this case, the work is done for us: the cartoonist called in a reporter some months later in order to make public some of the more unpleasant details of his private life, and in the course of the interview some light was shed on his own purposes, and on the purposes of his sponsors. He insisted on telling a yawning world that he had been through "eighty-five years of analysis where I had worked out my feelings toward [his mother]," that he was (in the words of his interviewer) still making "twice weekly visits to the same psychiatrist he has been seeing for years," that he had "lived with two different women during the past eleven years," and currently Shared His Life "with a woman he has lived with for a year and a half," and so on. The unattractiveness, in this case, was not so much in the dreary details of the life story, but in the telling of that story: the public exhibition of private confusion is almost always a dead giveaway. And sure enough, when he had finished gossiping about himself, Mr. Feiffer was eager to come clean. Some random but revelatory confessions: "I wanted to say all these terrible things about other Americans, but I want to rub their noses in it and have them love me for it." "I actually don't like any of these guys, no matter who they are." "The Reagan administration makes me angrier than I have been in a long time." "When [Lyndon Johnson] became a war criminal, he released my talent. It was fun because it was unbridled rage." "As awful as [Richard Nixon] was, he was a joy to go after." And so forth. Further analysis of Mr. Feiffer's personality would be superfluous and cruel.

Many historians maintain that the *Washington Post* finally touched bottom on the day the editors of the paper's "Style" section decided to entertain their stylish fans with a ghastly adolescent joke about the presumed cut of the future First Lady's underclothing. The joke—which had been overheard at a "sedate party" by a Californian journalist—was only the strangest part of a surrealist essay that had originally appeared in the *Los Angeles Herald Examiner* (there was no shortage of dirty newslinen in those final days), and on that memorable morning in November the guys at the *Post* pulled out all the stops and proceeded to reprint the whole gruesome piece, even the bit that made fun of the lady in question for her inability to tell sufficiently dirty stories. She left out the four-letter words, the prig. (It is worth noting that the article shared the mood of a scene that appeared shortly thereafter on the journalists' favorite television program—the work, mark it well, of the National Broadcasting Company—in which an actress playing another First Lady spoke the language of journalism—"it was either the election or the erection"—while disrobing on the president's desk.) The authors of the piece were no prudes, by God, and they forced themselves to write down one of the stories that the prissy Mrs. Reagan didn't like. Complete with dashes.

Still, even with the dashes, it was a Dionysian day for the last of the old culture, and only the very oldest members of the community could remember the time some seven years earlier when the executive editor of the *Washington Post* had been "stunned" (in the reporter Carl Bernstein's opinion) to hear that the Attorney General of the United States had made a vulgar remark about the executive editor's employer. Back in 1973, the editor just couldn't believe that such people really existed: "Was Mitchell drunk?" But no, it seemed that the Attorney General had not been drunk, and so the Stunned Editor had gone ahead and printed the remark, just to teach certain rude people a lesson. But, oddly enough, he refused to print the vulgar bit: he figured that "people would get the message" anyway—the message being, presumably, that vulgar souls were some-how unworthy souls. Which might have been true, but you wouldn't have known it in 1980: four weeks after her employees had been disseminating the singular suggestions about the next First Lady's intimate apparel, the publisher of the *Washington Post* invited her victim to be the guest of honor at a party (a "sedate" one, presumably), and Mrs. Reagan accepted.

The *Washington Post* was not unique in its some-what distorted view of existence; neither was it a worst case, or anywhere near it. Without generalizations, as Lady Montague said in one of her most generalizing letters, we would have nothing to talk about; but it should also be noted that any newspaper that had room for serious columnists and editors like George Will and Noel Epstein and William Raspberry and Meg Green-field and R. Emmett Tyrrell and Jonathan Yardley and for strictly honest and well-intentioned writers like Michael Barone and Colman McCarthy and Ken Ringle and for genuinely happy and whole-spirited people like Judith Martin and Henry Mitchell and Diana Mc-Clellan—to name just a few of the ladies and gentlemen in white hats of one sort or another—was a newspaper worth preserving. The notation is made with pleasure.

The *Post* was, however, one of the most interesting cases, from our point of view, because it was one of the most advanced—because the disease had spread to so many different parts of the organism. Indeed, it was a dangerous form of spiritual astigmatism precisely because it was so contagious. And if certain peculiar editorial obsessions could find their way into the

"Food" section of the paper—which was beginning to feature excerpts from impossibly funny diet books, explaining how to "dispel the effects of Saturday night celibacy" while achieving "richer orgasms"—then the book department, which was the department that mattered, didn't have a prayer.

What the book department did have was a well-educated but determinedly typical deputy editor named Michael Dirda, and even the stray volume of etymology wasn't safe from Mr. Dirda and the Grand Obsession: "I first turned my strictly scholarly attention to the risqué chapter," reported the Deputy, on the job as always. "Sadly—this is, as they say, a family newspaper—I must content myself with explaining the source of a single popular colloquial adjective" (what Mr. Dirda had in his hands was a perfectly innocent little word, but it had once had something to do with a particular digestive problem, and consequently it was just about the wildest thing he had ever come across, in his capacity as deputy editor). As for the rest of the book in question, well: "There's a lot more curious material nearby; interested readers should check out the backgrounds of *fornication*, *clitoris*, and *catamite*," said Mr. Dirda, doing his stuff for the specialized audience. He was fast, too: they handed him another volume, and he went straight to the good bit, which was all about a "vulgar term" for "part of a woman's anatomy." The deputy editor was a good man and a witty man and a clever man, but he had been too long at the *Post*: "Who said etymology couldn't be sexy?" cried the busy little intellectual.

No one had, unfortunately; and by the time the paper

got around to imitating the *Chicago Tribune* by reprinting an eight-page excerpt from Gay Talese's leaden examination of sex and Gay Talese, the battle was over. "It would be interesting," said a lonely little Letter to the Editor, "to know why the *Post* chose to publish the very long and dismally dull excerpt." There was no response, of course, partly because well-disguised Philistines don't ever talk about their sales charts in public, and partly because the editors already knew that the dam was about to break.

Sure enough, the muddy waters in the literary department suddenly spilled over the banks on the day the lame-duck Congress reconvened. That was the day the returning legislators opened their morning papers to discover a front-page review of a new Chinese sex manual.

"China's Latest Sex Manual Warns about Dangers of 'Hand Lewdness' " howled the subheadline; and indeed, it was apparently this Oriental distaste for the American cultural community's most popular form of "lewdness" that had so captivated the paper's literary and editorial mandarins. "In a nation that espouses socialist solidarity," chortled the *Post*, "the Communist Party talks an uncompromising stand against sexual self-gratification." "Masturbation," according to the *Post*, was "said to detract from one's work and study and ultimately cause impotence"—and so on and on, unto the second page. The kids didn't really approve of the new book, of course, ("terms such as foreplay and erogenous zones, which appear like landmarks in sexual manuals of the West, are conspicuously absent, as are the usual step-by-step exercises leading up to coi-

tus''), and they figured it wasn't sufficiently attentive to
something called ''female sexual equality'' (the manual
suggested that Chinese females liked ''a certain amount
of verbal romancing,'' which was not at *all* the way
things were done in the Thick Layer Of Journalism
That Was Young And Citified). But then, Chinese
folks, like so much of the rest of the world, seemed to be
hopelessly out of step with the Thick Layer: ''Premari-
tal sex has become a bit more common in recent years,
according to Chinese youth, although it is generally a
prelude to [gasp] marriage and rarely indulged in as a
simple pleasure.''

Suddenly, before anybody knew what was happening, the *Washington Post* had turned itself into Western
civilization, and Western Civilization knew there was
hope, even for Chinese puritans: ''While obviously old-
fashioned by Western standards, *Sexual Knowledge*
represents a real breakthrough in one of the world's
most puritanical nations.'' And if there were any new
fogies out there who were still nursing an unhealthy
interest in the work facing the Ninety-sixth Congress,
well, that just wasn't front-page stuff. Front-page stuff
had been described a few weeks earlier by the *Post*'s
plaintive resident pundit, Richard Cohen: ''No one
would argue that the various sex surveys have not
proven useful,'' he pleaded, with a disarming lack of
embarrassment; after all, ''the world has been made
better by what it has found out about sex—what people
do and with whom they do it.'' Also, the sexual conduct
of Mr. Cohen's fellow citizens was, um, ''an important
subject—at the very least, an obsession.''

Quite so.

The Thin Generation

The lives and attitudes of many younger American journalists (most of whom were in their late thirties or early forties) were pitiable enough, but the daily public exhibition of that pity was peculiarly dreadful. We are talking—not to put too fine a point on it—about some pretty stunted literary psyches. As a class, the journalistic vulgarians had never outgrown a postpubescent obsession with the clinical aspects of human behavior. They were still, as so many of them would have phrased it, "sexually hung up" on the mechanics of the process of reproduction; and because they still viewed the world through childhood's prism of physicality, they were utterly incapable of detecting the fragile beauty in the consummation of love, let alone the pathos in the consummation of lust. They were, in other words, psychological outsiders—ignorant of the deepest human emotions, and unable to share in one of the most universal of human understandings. As individuals, they were by definition mean of spirit and small of mind; as writers and cultural arbiters—as men and women of feeling and perception—they were imposters.

Are we looking at some unusually sleazy people here? You bet we are. But the judgment must be tempered: theirs, after all, was not the sleaze of intention, but of vacuity. It is the vacuity that makes the task of description and categorization so difficult: we are talking about a whole *class* of social misfits; but it was a class that eluded easy definition (if not instant recognition) precisely because it embodied no real beliefs, no standards, no purpose. It had only symptoms.

Who were these people, then? We name no names, we rule nobody out and nobody in; but by their habits ye shall know them. They were the people who talked about "alternative life-styles" and "bonding" and "parenting," the people who got excited about video games and video recorders and "surrogate mothers" and hot tubs, the people who read *Playboy* and *Playgirl* and *Cosmopolitan* and the *Village Voice*, the people who thought that "public discourse" was whatever had been on the cover of *Newsweek* that week. They were the people who referred to pornography as "adult entertainment," the people who buzzed about "television viewing experiences" and "enhancing relationships" and "sexuality," the people who wrote bizarre essays about the social tensions arising from "epidemics" of minor venereal diseases, the people whose thoughts and stories were littered with quotations from popular songs of the 1960s and references to movies new and old. They were the people who lamented the absence of trouble on American campuses ("apathy," they called the calm), the people who lit and fanned the fires of class hatred and bitterness because they needed company in their own distress, the people who were forever discovering non-existent "movements" that were "reminiscent of the Sixties," the people who prayed for excitement and conflict and crisis until the bricks started flying in their direction. They were the aging boys and girls who feared and rejected maturity because their world was the world of early adolescence, they were the sexually and emotionally crippled advocates of a society based on the principles of sophisticated whoredom, the bored disciples of mediocrity and envy and hopelessness and hate. We are talking about the cut-rate Freudians and the finger-snapping students of sexology and the moonlighting pop psychologists, about the creaking disco dancers and the sequential live-in lovers and the spiritually stunted losers of early middle age, about the aimless and bewildered victims of mass education whose lives were defined by comic strips and stereos and money and sex and *Rolling Stone* and the latest activities of their favorite film stars. We are talking about a very thin generation. We are talking about American journalism.

Specifically, we are talking about the lower-middle levels of American journalism—about the "cultural affairs correspondents" and the headline writers and the local columnists and the odd-jobbers who doubled as daily book reviewers. Their vulgarity was the vulgarity of emptiness; and if the serious American press was, as was often claimed by Europeans, the worst in the literate Western world, it was so not because its representatives believed in the wrong things, but because they believed in no thing.

The real danger lay twenty years in the future. The young vulgarians were relatively powerless in 1980, and their concerns were staggeringly trivial. The kids could still be brought to heel, or shamed into behaving themselves, or redirected, or—if all else failed—thrown out on their collective ear. But by the end of the century, if they had met with no significant opposition, they would have moved up to positions of genuine influence within their enclosure: they would be editing and assigning and pontificating and publishing, and helping to drag down what was left of their civilization with them. They might succeed; but it was much more likely that the destructive effort would so isolate the press from the educated classes that the fourth estate would become a complete irrelevance—with predictable consequences for the intellectual and political health of the republic.

They were merely victims, of course, maimed victims of the uncertainty that was part of the legacy of the eighteenth century to the twentieth. But victims can become as tyrants to the next generation.

Chapter *XIII*

Vulgarians of the Fourth Estate

A feeling of infinite melancholy afflicted me. How sad, how infinitely sad, all this was! In the Racine drug-store, it seemed to me, I was at the end of a long road. Havelock Ellis, D.H. Lawrence, H.G. Wells and many another pointed the way. Old Freud threw in his blessing, Kraft-Ebbing had a word to say, Wilhelm Reich was standing by with his orgone box. We were all to be happy as crickets in our freedom from past inhibitions and frustrations....

And now it had all ended in this sordid display of printed matter; not in Sodom or Gomorrah, but in Racine, Wisconsin; not in Byzantine scenes of debauchery, but in a drug-store; no vine leaves to put in the hair, but only hamburgers and ice-cream sundaes to swallow; no nymphs and satyrs, but only cheesecake, and the sad dreams of forlorn

166

lovers, solitary playboys, whose mistresses came
to them through the camera lens, that most ubiquitous of panders.

> Malcolm Muggeridge; on first looking
> into the books and periodicals displayed
> for sale in an American drug store.

As we have seen, the primitive doctrines of the tawdriest
of journalistic generations were celebrated even in the
pages of the oldest newspaper in the capital of the
largest English-speaking nation on earth. But the point
has also been made that the *Washington Post* was far
from being the worst of a rowdy lot, and that it still had
room for writers and editors who refused to participate
in the increasingly bizarre rituals of barnyard journalism. On the banks of the grand Potomac, the grunts of
the aging mudgods were incessant, but still not triumphant; lewd, but not quite obscene; indicative, but not
yet definitive. There were, in other words, lines that had
not yet been crossed.

The correlative and less pleasant point is that the
Post had plenty of company in the mad pursuit of
barbarity. The warp was pervasive, within the literary
community, and it was nationwide. What had begun as
an eccentric journalistic preoccupation with certain
universal physical processes had come in the end to
resemble the ritualistic snigger and wink of the senile
roué, as all the varied activity of the world, from politics
to science to art, was filtered through the prism of an
overstimulated and solitary erotic imagination.

As with all obsessive delusions, the prism of physicality was pitiful not for what it did see—sexual activity
still existed, in 1980, and so did all the normal proce-

dures of death and digestion and reproduction—but for what it did not see: which was all the truth and joy of human life. And—as with all such delusions—nothing was spared. John Simon published a new collection of short essays, and Carole Cook of the *Saturday Review* insisted that he was indulging in "literary coitus interruptus." The Republican Party won an election, and an editor at the *Washingtonian* magazine thought that the Party must be suffering from "post-coital sadness." Robert Penn Warren figured that the fall of a man from high position would always be greeted with "an orgasmic gasp of relief," the critic Alden Whitman thought that John D. Rockefeller's interest in mathematics was "virtually orgasmic," and the historian Paul Fussell wanted the world to know that travelling by ship was better than travelling by plane because "you can copulate" on a ship. A dance critic at *Newsweek* praised one sordid ballet for its "erotic atmosphere," which constituted "a spectacular orgy," and another critic at the same magazine reprimanded a singer who failed to deliver the essential "erotic energy." Two new biographies of Joan of Arc analyzed the Saint in terms of her "transvestism" and her "erotic energy" (one even devoted several paragraphs to the effects of horseback riding on virginity), and a reviewer for the *New York Review of Books* dismissed an old Victorian's memoirs because the author was far too vague about his "emergent sexuality": the old chap's "sexual primness" was annoying, and his book "lacked its one essential element, eroticism."

If there was a low point, it may have come when the boy who was the Education Editor of the *New York*

Times emerged from the swamp of higher education
with a "selective guide to colleges" that condemned
several of the nation's most respected universities for
being—and we quote, with near-disbelief—"sexually
uptight." Public Outrage (which was beginning to be
back in fashion) elicited an Official Statement from the
fifty-five-year-old publisher of the *Times*, Mr. Arthur
Ochs Sulzberger. Mr. Sulzberger felt that the use of his
newspaper's name in the title of the guide had been, uh,
"inappropriate," but he wanted to make it clear that
Sulzbergers were not prudes: the guide was "an excellent book that is based on solid reporting. We are
pleased to be publishing it."

There was a desperate ferocity in the air, as the professional journalistic vulgarians tried to beat the non-
erotic world to a pulp before they were dragged off the
stage. It could be seen between the lines when staffers at
United Press International applauded a well-known
American hotel chain for its plans to offer "pornographic movies and live shows" to refugees from "prudish"
African countries, and it was right out in front when the
editors of *Parade* magazine quailed before the thought
of "bluenose and Bible Belt boycotts" against actresses
who had "partaken in pornographic flicks." It was a
sign of the times that *Parade*'s plug for pornographic
actresses came in a column called "Keeping Up With
Youth": the fifty-year-old youths at *Parade* did *not* have
blue noses, please God, and they wanted to make damn
sure that genuine "Youth" didn't get one, either.

It was one of the faults of the American literary community that it made little distinction between the
"popular" press and the serious press. Still, if America

did have a popular press, *Parade* was it; and if the
hysteria had penetrated to the People's Sunday Sup-
plement, then the hysteria was everywhere. As if to
confirm that things would soon be out of control, the
editors of the magazine commissioned a most peculiar
piece from someone named Earl Ubell, who was a
"health and science editor" at a television station in
New York. For reasons best known to himself, Mr.
Ubell wanted "elderly people" to "upset an old taboo"
and start, um, whooping it up. It had come to Mr.
Ubell's attention that "more and more people abstain
from sex in each decade of life," and he didn't like it one
little bit. He couldn't understand it, for one thing: after
all, "if there is someone around who's caring, the physical act follows," doesn't it? Well, doesn't it? The bewildered television scientist contributed the obligatory
chatter about "sex-organ response," and some coy oohs
and ahs about "smooth, rounded bodies" and "tight,
rippling muscles," but it didn't take him long to get to
the point: he wanted older people to start "doing something sexual" pretty damn quick, especially if they
believed that "something" to be "improper, perhaps
even shameful." Why heck, if they would just *think*
about "doing it," they would prove to Mr. Ubell that
they possessed "a taste for adventure and variety."

And if Americans weren't interested in Mr. Ubell's
odd visions? If they resisted? Well, there were Certain
Methods: "Some people with declining sexual interest
may need help from a physician or a psychologist," said
Mr. Ubell mirthlessly. Regrettable, but necessary. In
other words, No More Mr. Nice Guy. Reeducation
might be required in certain cases: "Sometimes older

people—especially men—have to be retrained how to make love.... Partners also may have to be trained how to relax. If they have failed at sex, they may be anxious, and the more anxious they are, the more they will fail." And Mr. Ubell wouldn't like that. Not at all. Mr. Ubell didn't like people who Failed At Sex.

By the same token, when the reviewers made fun of her latest "erotic fantasy," the novelist Erica Jong struck out blindly at everybody else's "puritanical attitude." "I *knew* it would shock," said poor Ms. Jong, keeping her literary fingers crossed. Why, everybody but Ms. Jong thought that "sex was dirty." Oh hell, "it would take a whole generation to change that," grumbled the novelist, who—perhaps wisely—did not explain why she had decided to dedicate what remained of her life to the dead cause of universal eroticism. She was more precise a few months later, when she told an unaccountably inquisitive Anatole Broyard of the *New York Times Book Review* that "too many women writers try to get into men's gutters instead of finding their own." It was an attitude shared by a rival "feminist" novelist named Jill Robinson, who told the same interviewer: "I got into the gutter because I thought it would make me a better writer." But Ms. Jong had the last word: "Pretty soon Jill and I will be regarded as old fossils, with our passions, our raging, our tearing of our guts. We're advancing into venerability at an alarming rate."

Her despair was shared by the sixty-year-old "softporn" publisher Maurice Girodias, who just knew that all of *his* troubles were "rooted in Puritanism." He was very much afraid that the New Mood had "damaged

literature and the evolution of the intellectual community," which was his way of saying that the new
mood had put an end to the evolution of Maurice Girodias's literary reputation. Just like Ms. Jong, Mr. Girodias was pretty sure that most other people thought that
"sex has to be very dirty."

It was a primitive—almost a prehistoric—complaint,
and it was being uttered in increasingly strident tones
by everyone from the *Washington Post* columnist
Richard Cohen—who was anxious to reassure himself
that citizens who disapproved of sex education in the
public schools *really* thought that "sex itself" was
somehow "dirty"—to the University of California's resident sexologist, who was just as sure that "the moral
majority" was "clearly anti-sex." For years, the self-
righteous eroticians had tried to bully literature and
society into meek compliance, and they just couldn't
stop: like all bullies, they didn't know any other way of
doing business.

The aging planners of the orgiastic order could not—
would not—understand that their sordid authority was
being taken away. After all, they reasoned, the decks
were still littered with previous victims, maimed writers
and critics and editors and readers who could not yet
believe that it was finally safe for them to get up and
start walking as humans again, and grown-up humans
at that.

One of those who was still down was poor Margaret
Truman Daniel, the daughter of the former President
and the wife of the former managing editor of the *New
York Times*. Ms. Truman had written a new book, and
it hadn't been easy. "I had problems writing the sex

scenes," said the fifty-five-year-old mother of four. "But I had to get over that. My publisher made a lot of good suggestions." Publishers' suggestions made for strange bedfellows in those days, and Ms. Truman had an unlikely ally in the political philosopher William F. Buckley. For half a century Mr. Buckley had been making his own rules (and his rules were some of the best), but when he started writing novels of espionage he was careful to "put in the OSS—the Obligatory Sex Scenes" (the phrase had been passed to him by the author of *Lolita*). The Truman-Buckley alliance had its ironies: twenty years earlier Mr. Buckley had quite properly reprimanded Ms. Truman's parent for "cavorting from vulgarity to vulgarity," and for "provoking base appetites." The elder Truman had been a "conspicuous vulgarian," and Mr. Buckley had suggested that the failure of good and civilized men to "stand firm" in resistance to such public vulgarity "would seem to lead to an anarchy in the world of taste and judgment." Right again.

William F. Buckley and Margaret Truman are not being criticized here. On the contrary: the point is that they were *not* vulgarians, in any sense of the word. They were the best: the finished product of two thousand years of Western culture, well-educated and well-intentioned and well-mannered, the "last best hope" of civility. They were, in other words, just about as good—and as lucky, in some ways—as we get; and if they could not "stand firm" in the defense of absolute literary civility and public virtue, then nobody could. And that was the great social evil in the anarchy of taste and judgment: that it intruded upon and gradually defiled genuine love and affection and principle and decency. The *Newsweek*s and the *Playboy*s and the *Village Voice*s had been pouring their dismal crudities over real people for so many dreary years that some of the stuff had begun to stick. The best people and the best loves and the best friendships and the best intentions had been soiled because the best men and women had tolerated and eventually sanctioned the dissemination of the sickly fantasies of the worst. Literature and public discourse were but incidental casualties: all human association and all sweet aspiration had been soured and stained by the rank fluid of the professional vulgarians, until finally healthy men and women were afraid to look one another in the eye, lest they should discover that their hearts too had been cheapened and diminished by the doctrine and the disciples of animalism; afraid to stand alone in protest, lest they be accused of "prudery" or "Victorianism" or "naïveté" or "intolerance"; reluctant to cry enough, for fear there was more to come.

Before it was all over, the critic Walter Clemons of *Newsweek* was to be heard confessing that he was completely bewildered by the friendship between the blind humanitarian Helen Keller and her tutor 'Anne Sullivan: "Since there is not the slightest hint of any sexual warmth between them, it is a wonder they didn't grow to hate each other." He really said it. Indeed, for reasons not to be probed, Mr. Clemons was oddly eager to reassure himself that Miss Keller was not "the sexless Goody two-shoes her genteel public expected her to be." People like that made Mr. Clemons feel uncomfortable, he couldn't say just why. They were so Goddamn *good*, you know? Almost as though they knew something about life that Mr. Clemons didn't. Like a disproportionate number of his colleagues, Mr. Clemons was just fifty years old in 1980, and he couldn't bear the thought that he might have missed out on some elementary truth along the way, some truth that might make it possible for two women to be friends with each other and stay out of bed at the same time. Mr. Clemons was either going to have to start learning about life all over again, or he was going to have to stick his fingers in his ears and repeat the old shibboleths until the awful truth went away. In those days, only very exceptional fifty-year-olds had the courage to choose the first option.

To be fair to the crew at *Newsweek*, it should be said that they had a lot of stiff competition from *Time* magazine. It was the critic R.Z. Sheppard of *Time*, after all, who cheered one novel that "managed to churn a few stomachs," and who found it necessary to explain that soldiers didn't like war primarily because their "arms, legs, eyes and genitals" were threatened. Which was about what one would have expected from a reviewer who thought of all war as "the great deflowerer of youth." It was also about what one would have expected from the magazine that had devoted several columns to a giggly little dissertation on sexual fantasies in the land of journalism, a magazine that had given America a quick peek into a frightened editorial heart when it insisted that "forced-sex fantasy...is one of the most common sexual daydreams of American women." The boys and girls had been reading Masters and Johnson again (only reporters actually *read* all the sex guides), not to mention someone named Nancy

Friday, and they were especially excited about some new "sadistic fantasies." They chattered happily about how to have plenty of orgasms, and about "the fantasy of performing oral sex," and about all the other crucial issues that were keeping the lower echelons of the literary community afloat in the final third of the century. "Men want women more than women want men," thundered *Time*.

It was not so odd that young reporters and critics and editors should be passing around a pamphlet by a former "sex-fantasy columnist for a girlie magazine," and it was not so odd that the same reporters and critics and editors should jump at the chance to produce turgid little essays about the rules of cunnilingus and fellatio; but it was exceedingly odd that those reporters and critics and editors—and those essays—should be associated with what had once been the Nation's Weekly Newsmagazine.

Under the circumstances, nobody was too astonished when *Time* began to run full-color, three-column photographs of bare-breasted strippers (complete with kicky "black stockings and garter belt"), and few jaws dropped when the magazine's cultural essayists ended their policy of détente with the Soviet Union because they could no longer stomach "the woeful sexual lives of most Soviet Citizens." The diplomatic freeze was regrettable but necessary: the wretched Soviet Citizens were "overwhelmed by long entrenched sexual myths" and that was pretty bad. Why, the Soviet government seemed to "deny the very idea of a sex life," puffed *Time*, growing positively red (and white and blue) in the face. Why good God, man, there was "repression and prudishness" wherever you looked in that Godless Russian land, and that was a *fact*, "a sad fact." "Sex therapy clinics are nonexistent," and *Time* had reason to believe that it wasn't *true* that "one hundred percent of Soviet men reach orgasm." Oh, the horror of Leninism. Not only that, but the Typical Russian Sex Act was performed in the dark! In bed! Under...under the bedclothes! "Foreplay," said *Time*'s ashen authority, was "virtually unheard of." Pretty soon the kids at *Time* were down on their hands and knees with a crayon: "Typically, the female assumes what the Russians call the crayfish position with head and knees touching the bed," explained the heirs of Luce. "Her partner penetrates from the rear, and usually dismounts quickly." And—don't go away, *please* don't go away—Soviet men refused to hold "back an ejaculation to satisfy the woman"! No wonder the cads went into Afghanistan, we here at *Time* should have seen it coming.

But as always, what had begun as an absurd effort to titillate the sales charts ended in ugly bitterness, and pretty soon *Time*'s kids were taking aim at Russian "restraint." "Except for prostitution, which continues to flourish [all is not lost] in spite of official efforts to wipe it out, the Soviets have no stomach for 'deviant' behavior. Pornography is rare. Oral sex is performed only with prostitutes (out of male fears of venereal disease). Popular scorn of homosexuality is so intense that it is 'simply passed over in silence.' "

Silence. Restraint. Discretion. *That's* what the cultural community couldn't stand, all that restraint out there, all that horrible, horrible control. As if Having A Stomach For Oral Sex weren't just about the most important thing in all the world! Still, "Some efforts seem to be under way to break away from the stifling past. There is, for instance, a fledgling underground pornographic press," said *Time* hopefully. Also, the author of something called *Sex in the Soviet Union* (published by Times Books, of course) had revealed that "daring protesters have been dropping pornographic doodles into ballot boxes," and that was encouraging (almost like Literary Life in the good old USA). But "in spite of such pathetic signs of rebellion," the expert did "not see enlightenment any time soon," and that was not so encouraging. *Time* did not go so far as to demand that Radio Free Europe start directing pornographic broadcasts at the Russian people in order to further the cause of "enlightenment," but that was only because the whole thing seemed so futile all of a sudden: the expert feared that "sex may become increasingly cold, cynical and impersonal in the U.S.S.R.," and the future didn't look so rosy for certain journalistic reputations back in the States, either.

A few weeks later, the publisher of *Time* tried to save the situation without tripping over his trenchcoat in the process. "For journalists, caught up in the swirl of fast-breaking events, it is sometimes easy to neglect the longer view, to forget the lessons of history," he muttered, trying not to sound overly dramatic about the whole thing. It was a pretty flimsy excuse. And if the swirl of fast-breaking events had had anything at all to do with the fast-breaking fantasies of oral sex that had been decorating his publication in recent weeks, the Publisher wasn't saying. He had a swirl to catch.

But *Time*'s crisis management team sensed a change

in the wind, and they were nervous. The guys tried to put a brave face on their worries, of course: a Senior Writer named Lance Morrow was sent out to assure the troops that all the reports of "a kind of counterrevolution" by the "aggressively wholesome" had been "much exaggerated." Mr. Morrow (who was in fact more talented and much more thoughtful than many of his colleagues) had to admit that "large numbers of Americans are sick of a society in which so many standards of conduct have collapsed," but he was there to say that the patriots of *Time* would have no truck with the "militant moralism" of fundamentalist movements. All in all, he sounded a lot like that very model of a modern Senior Writer Frank Trippett, who, we recall, wanted to stamp out "the resurgent moralistic mood" (and, not so incidentally, make sure that the novels of Ken Kesey were approved for study in the schools of Idaho Falls).

Alas, the boys never got the chance to stamp. They were bowled over in mid-hop by their very own Editor-in-Chief, Henry Grunwald, who came charging into the cultural theater like a moralist possessed, issuing calls right and left for—who would have guessed it—"a resurgence of values." "We face a crisis of moral responsibility," thundered Mr. Grunwald, trying very hard to sound like the sort of fellow who'd never even *heard* of Senior Writers, the sort of fellow who would never have tolerated a series of essays on male sex fantasies, who would have resigned rather than run a full-color spread on nude strippers. As a matter of fact, Mr. Grunwald was suddenly fed up to *here* with the "excesses of the Sixties and Seventies," and he, at least, had noticed just in time that people—"especially the young"—had

"begun to rediscover a desperate need for standards."
The Editor-in-Chief was positively awful in his rediscovered majesty: he demanded a new "code of secular
morality," not to mention a little "respect for authority," please, and also "a sense of duty, and a degree of
self-restraint." Oddly enough, *Time*'s moralizing
Vigilante-in-Chief didn't see any place for "moralizing
vigilantes" in the new order: on the contrary, the new
Utopia would be the result of "millions of individual
decisions and efforts," and it was suddenly okay for
everybody—including, presumably, those scary people
who sat on the school book review committees of Idaho
Falls—to pull up their socks and "take up their responsibilities" again.

It was a stirring moment in the history of cultural
trend-spotting, but there was an embarrassed silence in
at least one corner of the stage. Mr. Grunwald hadn't
said a *word* about deviant sexual fantasies or the novels
of Ken Kesey, and certain bewildered staffers looked
lonelier than ever.

An editor in chief (as distinct from a managing editor) cannot be blamed for every bit of bad or antisocial
writing that appears in his or her publication; but he or
she may be blamed for patterns of bad or irresponsible
writing that become apparent over a period of weeks or
months—if only because the development of any given
pattern implies that several opportunities to call a halt
to that development have been passed up (writers have
not been reprimanded, assistant editors have not been
warned, etc.). Henry Grunwald's failure to fulfill his
responsibilities as the guiding conscience of a serious

journal of opinion—his refusal, that is, to tell the kids to cut it out—lent a hollow tone to his insistence that his fellow citizens take up *their* responsibilities.

But if we have made some fun of Henry Grunwald's call for a renewed sense of purpose—and we have—the fun has been aimed not at the preacher, but at the practice. Which is to say that Mr. Grunwald himself was a good and decent man, and that his essay was a thing of rare magnificence and honor in a dismal time. The cheers, in this instance, are louder—much louder—than the laughs; and *Time* magazine was in much better shape than much of the competition.

Last Taxi

Unfortunately, it is much easier to fall into a hole than it is to climb out of one, and the staffers at *Time* hadn't even stopped falling yet. They didn't hit bottom—and even then, it may have been a false bottom—until the autumn of 1981; but when they hit, they hit hard.

As so often before, a new motion picture served as catalyst: it was a hard-core pornographic film called *Taxi to the Toilet* (for obvious reasons, its American distributors retained the original German title, *Taxi zum Klo*), and it featured a "gay activist" named Frank Ripploh. Pamela Hansford Johnson once spoke for many people when she said that she wished "someone would lay down guide lines between what is soft, and what is hard," but sometimes there is no doubt. According to Gary Arnold of the *Washington Post*, the film made no bones about its purposes: it constituted, he said, a paean to "sordid hardcore sex," including "one interlude of rough interplay whose kinkiness might be politely described as repulsive." As promised, most of the action took place in latrines, and that action was succinctly described by Stanley Kauffman of the *New Republic*: "Ripploh and friends do their fellating in plain sight. And Ripploh can't resist showing us— often—his anus, on one pretext or another. No hetero-sexual film that I know, outside porn, has dared to do these things or their equivalents."

Had the merchants of sleaze gone too far at last? Was this the picture that would finally open a million jaded eyes? Not a bit of it. "Witty, charming, rigorously unsentimental," gushed Richard Corliss of *Time*, who didn't want to hear any arguments from prisoners of "prudery" (i.e., non-journalists) and others who were unaccountably persisting in their "resistance to explicit sex in mainstream movies." Mr. Corliss—an Associate Editor of the weekly newsmagazine, let us note—*liked* all those delicious wide-screen shots of Mr. Ripploh's excretory opening (Mr. Ripploh was, after all, "a film maker of promise and achievement"), and he just couldn't wait for some sequels: "*Taxi* is a big step toward liberating the screen."

Kauffman of the *New Republic* had Mr. Corliss's number: "What makes the frankness in *Taxi* especially unacceptable is that the eagerness to call it a comedy and the lack of objections to its explicitness seem to indicate less breadth of spirit and Rabelaisian gusto than bourgeois nervousness at being thought prudish."

In one of those little ironies so characteristic of con-temporary journalism, the same issue of *Time* that carried Mr. Corliss's somewhat hysterical call for more flesh also carried a well-aimed attack on the *Washington Post* by one of *Time*'s "Contributors." The Contributor (Thomas Griffith) was particularly distressed by one of the *Post*'s "leering" accounts of a public figure's "sexual behavior": "The *Post* is a schizoid newspaper—solid in its reporting of national and international affairs, flashy in feature sections where writers are encouraged to stretch their imaginations."

The same might have been said not only of *Time* itself but of most of the American popular press. All over the land of the free, hip little film critics were celebrating the exhibition of Mr. Ripploh's lower orifices with the words and phrases they'd memorized while studying for their Master's degrees. "The latest film to assault the barrier between pornography and art," giggled David Ansen of *Newsweek*, who figured it would be a damn "shame if the shock value blinded viewers to the film's high-spirited, disarmingly honest soul." "A landmark in its unself-conscious and unretouched depiction of the fast-lane homosexual experience," sighed young David, who was all agog at "some of the more outré expressions of Sadomasochism," which were, oh *goody*, "presented graphically and with no psychological gloss." Sure, it was all "as explicit as any porn movie," but, ahem, "in this context," understand, "the sex is a form of honest reportage," almost as honest—and as Real—as movie reviewing. "The man's a filmmaker," sobbed Mr. Ansen, trying to hang onto what was left of his dignity without losing sight of the screen.

And so it went. "Self-awareness of an unusually high

order," buzzed Vincent Canby of the *New York Times*, adjusting his blinders to get a better look. "An important movie," sniffed one critic at the *Village Voice*; "the first masterpiece about the mainstream of male gay life!" shrieked another. I mean the whole office was just so *excited*. "A believable and touching portrait," wept Janet Maslin of the *New York Times*, trying to sound just like one of the boys, and succeeding. Perhaps Mr. Corliss of *Time* went back for a second look; in any case, he resurfaced in the pages of *Film Comment*, and he was beginning to sound a bit shrill: "Ripploh is the movies' future," he cried anxiously. "It will be interesting to see how this *Taxi* runs on our own mean streets," said he, and you can bet he felt pretty tough underneath his grey flannel. As for Archer Winsten of the *New York Post*, he *did* go back for a second helping: "Seeing it a second time, I was surprised by my own reaction. It seemed less shocking."

Precisely. That's the evil in it, of course: you get used to it, after a while. And then it's hard to break the habit. You cannot—as an individual or as a publication or a nation—demean yourself for months or years on end and then suddenly decide you've had enough. In the early 1980s, certain people had a long-standing investment in what used to be called "filth": they could not wipe it from their hands without rejecting their own pasts and their own behavior, as writers and as humans. That was Henry Grunwald's difficulty: if you let a boy like Richard Corliss misbehave once, in print, he's going to misbehave again, if only to justify his previous shame to himself.

The late Lady Snow (Pamela Hansford Johnson)

identified the problem back in 1966, in an article written for *Life* magazine:

> Under the big top of the all-permissive, "swinging society" we have the whole garish circus of the New Freedom—freedom to revel, through all kinds of mass media, in violence, in pornography, in sado-masochism. Walls of the police storerooms bulge outwards with the pressure of tons upon tons of dirty books—the ones within the scope of the law. But there are plenty outside its scope, so our libertarian intellectuals, who are the new tyrants, are not worrying just yet.
>
> It is quite difficult to ask even a simple question about the whole problem of license today—such as, "Is what we are doing socially harmful? Because of it, do some people get hurt?"—and get a sober answer. Such a question usually prompts only the most unthinking tantrums, as if a child were clutching to its breast some precious, grubby toy rabbit with which it cannot bear to part.

And she identified the danger as well:

> We are, I think, in danger of creating a society lacking in what the psychologists call *affect*—that is, any capacity for entering into the feelings of others. Nobody cares for anyone but himself, or for anything but instant self-gratification. We demand sex without love, we demand violence for "kicks." We are encouraging the blunting of sensibility; and this, let us remember, has not been the way to an earthly paradise but the way to Auschwitz.

Death Watch

But how had the sons and daughters of artistic and

moral license arrived at their dreary station in life to begin with? After all, their feverish embrace of animalism—and secondhand animalism at that—was an unnatural embrace. At any time in the twenty-five hundred years that built the Western culture, citizens might have chosen to abandon their façades of civility and humanity, and deface their newspapers and their libraries and their public squares with repetitive diagrams of the most basic procedures of digestion and death and reproduction (after all, American writers in the twentieth century didn't feel anything that Victorians and Macedonians hadn't felt); but no significant culture—not even the most primitive—had ever wanted to exercise that easiest of options. The twentieth century witnessed a return to prehistorical attitudes in such matters, and by 1980 it had become axiomatic that mechanical diagrams of the elemental acts were manifestations of "art" or "literature," rather than of plumbing or pornography or animal husbandry or mental disease; and that the description and the discussion of the acts and the diagrams was a form of "journalism." The question was—how?

How had the kids become so isolated from human history and purpose, and so divorced from normal emotion and experience? How had they come, in their own poor hearts, to equate "art" with enormous technicolor pictures of—forgive us—a troubled German's anus? What bitterness spurred them on to savage their own society and their own happiness? Why did they want so desperately to see their children, and the children of their friends, grow up in the world defined and surrounded by films of fellatio and pictures of human excretory organs? What was their sickness, and how had it got into them?

In 1981, a doctor at the Menninger School of Psychiatry told a congressional subcommittee that the professional sexualists were "militant, rebellious, personally and sexually disturbed individuals." It was only a partial explanation. After all, every era in human history has had its share of sexual, psychological, and spiritual cripples. In some periods these unfortunates were constrained in their behavior and their speech by the will (and the law) of the healthy majority; in others (most recently the Victorian) by their own consciences as well. Very occasionally one of these individuals ascended to a position of authority in the field of his disability, but most of them were consigned—sometimes by reason of their disability, but more often by reason of their personal mediocrity or economic circumstance—to the ranks of the masses, where their opportunity to do harm to the society as a whole was severely restricted. It was only in the twentieth century that the human misfits began to ascend to positions of cultural influence by *virtue* of their personal and intellectual deficiencies.

The phenomenon was in part merely an unpleasant by-product of mass education: a man who might have done no harm as a head footman a century or two ago can do tremendous harm as an assistant professor or a film critic; and the people who might have been head footmen in a previous era were precisely the people who became professors and critics in 1980. In that sense, the disease was another symptom of the celebration of demos—the mediocre crowding out the excellent, simply because there were more of the former than of the latter.

But it is not enough to say that the masses had risen, and to leave it at that. The truth about the masses is that they are—like the elites—composed of a pretty nice bunch of well-meaning folks who want only to lead quiet and happy lives. The proportion of actual good to evil does not vary much, from class to class: the great mass of any group will always be pretty decent, given half a chance. Not particularly talented or large-spirited, perhaps, and certainly not particularly intelligent, but decent. How did it happen, then, that the artistic and journalistic arenas were occupied, so quickly and so easily, by guerrillas from the most unsavory quarters of society?

The short answer is that the vulgarians occupied the cultural stations because they wanted to and because they could. They could because the gospel of egalitarianism allied with mass education had made the move possible: for the first time in history, it was possible for human misfits to exercise an influence on their society *as a unit*. In the democratic century, an average man or woman with average (or greater than average) personal problems could set up shop as an "artist" or a "critic" or a "film maker" or a "reporter," and be listened to, or at least tolerated, by other average men and women. The vulgarians realized this, and—individually and collectively—resolved to concentrate their energies in the cultural districts, which had been left largely unprotected since the deaths of the last of the Victorian giants.

And *why* did the vulgarians want to exert such a powerful influence on their culture? For the obvious reason: they were envious of whole-souled men and women, and jealous of the human spirit. Because they were bewildered by the deepest human emotions and aspirations—because they had no conception of what it was that men and women had been talking about and playing at for all those centuries—they *had* to remake the society if their own lives were to have any meaning. It is a natural human instinct to try to appease one's confusions by pretending that they are not confusions at all, but virtues. People who cannot share in the common human spirit resent that spirit when they see it in others, and seek to destroy it, that they may feel whole themselves.

We are not, of course, suggesting that every one of the strident professional vulgarians was (in the words of the Menninger psychiatrist) "personally and sexually disturbed." On the contrary: it is possible, even probable, that many of them were fundamentally ordinary people—which is to say that it is possible that many of them were mere followers (and victims) of a trend. But what we can be sure of is that we are talking about some very unhappy people: idle and over-educated products of peace and prosperity and television, legions of prematurely flabby "journalists" and "social scientists" and "artists" with no genuine beliefs and no purpose in life, the bored progeny of plenty who took their emotions from popular songs of the 1960s and their understanding of the world from actors who played journalists on television, half-humans who frittered away their long lives chattering about the mechanics of sex and show business simply because they had nothing else to do.

They were products of the electronic age, and they lived electronic lives. When a comedian who had appeared for a few years on one of their most admired

and most disreputable television series died unexpect-
edly of a drug overdose, it was thrilling front-page news
in Major Papers all over the nation, because it was
thrilling front-page news in the dreams of middle-aged
journalists all over the nation (by contrast, when one of
the most controversial philosophers of the century died
the following day, the news was buried in the obituary
pages). The problem, of course, was that the journalists
didn't *want* to be middle-aged: they wanted to be children. Middle age implied maturity; and the concerns of
maturity did not include the television toys of childhood. Our chosen specimen (the *Washington Post*)
genuinely believed that the late television actor had
commanded a "huge and adoring audience," by which
the paper meant that he had "attained a vast popularity
among teen-agers and his 20- and 30-year-old contemporaries." Our point exactly (though if the starry-eyed
journalists had actually spoken to genuine youth—
especially serious youths—instead of trying to imitate
an obsolete and never-very-accurate image of youth,
they would have received something of a shock, and a
disdainful glance or two as well). The ladies and gentlemen of the fourth estate really thought that the obscure young television comedian had been a major force
in his time: "Discussions and imitations of his roles and
routines became conversational staples in broad segments of American society," claimed the *Post* with a
straight face; and if we substitute "the city room" for
"broad segments of American society," the sentence
says it all. It was a tiny, ingrown world that thought it
was a big world, and its boundaries were defined by one
of the *Post*'s regular columnists, as he spoke of the late

actor in the hushed tones formerly reserved for the heroes of Marathon:

> He could not be casually encountered; he will not be casually forgotten.... He came and went like a comet, but no one will ever have to wonder if he was here. He was here all right. He was here.

The pathetic truth, of course, was that "he" *hadn't* been "here." He had been on television, telling off-color jokes to cameras.

So we are talking, in the final analysis, about losers: about people who defined themselves and their world in terms of the lowest common human denominators—sexual congress and popular entertainment—because it was only within that context that they could discover any stimulation at all. They worshipped at the twin altars of animality and entertainment primarily because the ceremony of worship gave them something to do with themselves while they waited—for so many long, long years—for their pointless lives to be over. They were the people we had been predicting for two centuries, and they had finally arrived: the victims of political, economic, and scientific advance, the blameless heirs of utilitarianism and rationalism and existentialism and equalitarianism and rugged individualism. They were the dark face of progress; and they were losers because they had lost themselves.

Professor Duncan Williams spoke of their predicament, in his book *Trousered Apes*:

> Basically, I have no quarrel with...views which uphold the substitution of individual (i.e., internal) standards for the old-fashioned, legalistic and external ones. There is, however, a very real

danger in the *popularization* of such ideas. Self-fulfillment demands a certain measure of restraint, of self-control. This is an adult concept, as I think even its exponents would agree; and in between those two plateaux, the old morality and the new self-fulfillment (or "self-actualization") there exists a chasm into which, while attempting to cross, the majority falls. This chasm is self-indulgence, a descent to mere animal gratification, which presents the greatest danger to the immature who, vaguely aware of the demise of the old sanctions, delight in the permissiveness which increasingly pervades our society.

In chronicling the adventures of various journalistic vulgarians—and the effects of those adventures upon innocent parties—we have not been digressing from our larger theme. The journalistic disease was often dismissed as just another symptom of the widespread intellectual uncertainty, but in truth it was one of the causes of that uncertainty as well. As we have seen, the manic democratization of Western culture had gradually eroded the natural barriers between serious literature and popular entertainment. With that erosion came the confusion and eventually the destruction of the ancient intellectual hierarchies. In the second half of the twentieth century, the old excuses for irresponsible journalism—"we are only the messengers of bad news," "we mirror Reality," etc.—concealed about as much truth as the newer excuse for bad art ("the Art is bad because The Times are bad"); which is to say, not much truth at all. In the formless culture, lacking overt hierarchies, there was no longer any clearly-defined social "reality" to mirror; so the popular press made up its own reality—usually in the image of itself—and wrote about that instead. Agents of the Fourth Estate were still maintaining, as they had for centuries, that journalism was defenseless against random artistic and social perversity; but it would have been more to the point to concede that society (and art) had become vulnerable to every passing journalistic sickness. It was no longer possible to quarantine moral or intellectual rot—no longer possible to restrict any given germ of decay to one element or quarter of society, where it might be isolated and fought. That is why it is appropriate—even essential—to examine the journalistic offenders, witting and unwitting, within the context of the larger literary and cultural collapse; and that is why the antics of a relatively small band of spiritual and emotional pygmies would haunt and embarrass the entire culture for decades to come.

In other words, the civilization had no control group, no check and no balance—no stable extragovernmental community capable of drawing the necessary lines and honoring and protecting commonly-agreed-upon standards of civilized behavior and discourse. In healthier times, that regulatory function had been one of the natural responsibilities of the citizenry at large, and in particular of the leading citizens of every district— "community standards," it used to be called. But legal authority—popularly known as "the judges"—had withdrawn that responsibility from the citizenry. Unfortunately, The Judges had forgotten to give it to anyone else. The responsibility had been assumed for several decades by the more visible members of national and local government, and some of the last people to believe in sanctions and standards had entered public service; but now the credibility and authority of those figures was under increasing attack, both from within government (by the same tides of aimless legalism and moral rot and suicidal democratization that had dissolved the larger culture), and from without—by the forces of envy and ignorance and distrust and journalism. What was left of civilization in 1980 was virtually rudderless.

The "breakdown of standards" (so lamented by those agents of the popular press who were not busy breaking down standards) was not an unpleasant side-effect of an overdose of pure democracy, but part of the *definition* of democracy. There can be no standards, where there are no standard-setters.

The befuddled humanists had given pure cultural democracy a very good try—and truly their effort *was* one of the noblest social experiments of modern times—but the odds had been too great. Humans, after all, were only humans; and the great mass of men would always require just a little outside help—moral, intellectual, and behavioral—if its constituent members were to lead true and happy lives without smashing up themselves and their civilization in the process. The noble experiment seemed to be ending as a monstrous practical joke: as a society of unimaginably free people who couldn't think of anything to do with their freedom; a society of free people who couldn't remember why they had wanted to be free; a society of free people who were standing around waiting for someone to tell them how to behave. After two hundred years of effort, the disciples of Rousseau had finally created the ultimate social paradox: a dictatorship of liberty.

In those final days, some were beginning to realize, at last, that humans were truly equal on only two levels: the lowest, and the highest. But the realization had come too late. And because the social planners had not pointed the way to the highest—the angel—they had led the way to the lowest: the beast. They had made a jungle, and called it fair.

Chapter XIV

Literary Passions

We were more than shocked, we were angered
and saddened. Since here we recognized the
Enemy—that creeping infection of vulgarity that
will subdue the world. Like the sand of Arizona it
seeps stealthily, obliterating our ancient monuments and temples, filling even our gardens with
its gritty dust.

It was the loud applause with which the passengers greeted the exhibition that was so depressing. Probably none of them, as individuals, approved of the action; but as a mass audience they
were moved to assent.

Sir Harold Nicolson

All exhibitionism—physical, emotional, intellectual or
moral—is by definition vulgar, but the last literary
debauch of the worn-out cultural government was, at
least in its final stages, an unusually and deliberately

196

squalid affair. By exposing their mounting mental and emotional hysteria to public view, the literary strippers hoped to reestablish the essential distinction between "art" and the rest of the culture; and "art," in those mad times, was the stuff that was just a little more prurient and a little uglier than everything else.

The novelist E.F. Benson (among many others) had imagined the shape of 1980 back in 1919, as he traced the deadly shape of a fictional literary opportunist who had stumbled over an ancient evil and mistaken it for "a new aspect of the world": "Where before the enchantment of life moved him, he felt now only the call of putrefaction and decay. The lethal side of the created world had become exquisite in his eyes, and the beauty of it was derived from its everlasting corruption, not from the eternal upspringing of life. Lust, not love, was the force that kept it young, and renewed it so that the harvest of its decay should never cease to be reaped." The soul of Benson's literary jackal had become "a mirror that distorted into grotesque and evil shapes every image of beauty that was reflected in it, and rejoiced in them; it seemed to him that all nature, as well as all human motive, was based upon this exquisite secret that he had discovered."

And yet there was a difference between the imaginary jackals of 1919 and the actual scavengers of the late 1970s and early 1980s. Benson's fictional author was still reluctant to describe his ancient sickness with what he thought of as "bald realism." On the contrary, he resolved to

wrap his message up in a sort of mystic subtlety so
that only those who had implanted in them the
true instinct should be able to fill their souls with
the perfume of his flowers. Others might guess
and wonder and be puzzled, and perhaps see so far
as to put down his book with disgust that was still
half incredulous; but only the initiated would be
able to grasp wholly the message that lurked in his
hints and allusions.

But the artistic thugs of 1980 lived in less restrictive
times, and they had no need—and therefore, they
thought, no use—for hints and allusions. The kids were
out of the stifling closet of civilization at last, and eager
to go public with the lethal secret that was always being
rediscovered.

The old pornographer Henry Miller had given them
their stage directions as long ago as 1961, some twenty
years before he finally left the world to the mercies of his
intellectual progeny. "You see," Mr. Miller explained,

civilized peoples don't live according to moral
codes or principles of any kind. We speak about
them, we pay lip service to them, but nobody
believes in them. Nobody practices these rules,
they have no place in our lives. Taboos after all are
only hangovers, the product of diseased minds,
you might say, of fearsome people who hadn't the
courage to live and who under the guise of morality and religion have imposed these things upon
us.

Like so many of his artistic descendants, Mr. Miller
was utterly incapable of quitting while he was still in
control of himself. "The word 'civilization' to my mind
is coupled with death. When I use the word, I see civilization as a crippling, thwarting thing, a stultifying

thing. For me it was always so." "Civilization," hissed the old mountebank, "is the arteriosclerosis of culture."

It had been a pathetic hiss in 1961; it had become a convenient cover by the time of the great literary and cultural madness. As the former intellectual community slid further and further into a kind of twilight zone of psuedo-literacy, what the *Washington Post* had referred to as "an important subject"—"what people do and with whom they do it"—began to function as a rather rickety lifeboat for professors and critics and editors and booksellers and publishers adrift on the seas of intellectual confusion.

It was an almost surrealistic experience, in the dusk of the nuclear era, to see grown men and women struggling tearfully to duplicate and popularize the perceptions of a psychologically troubled thirteen-year-old. The scramble—not to put too fine a point on it—was more than a little weird: from the former editor in chief of the house of Putnam ("I adore good pornography") to the former president of the Olympia Press (who was championing "healthy eroticism") to the extraordinarily supple "cultural affairs correspondent" of the *New York Times* ("in some fictional scenes you must write with your emotions and your genitals") to the former director of the Metropolitan Museum of Art ("like it or not, pornography is part of the artistic spectrum") all the way down to the director of the University of California's Sex Counseling Unit (yes, the University of California really had a Sex Counseling Unit)—who was advising bookish Americans to read hard-core pornography because "like it or not, men and women often respond to pornography"—the pack was scrabbling for space in one of literary history's most peculiar schools of thought.

A spokesman for the publishing house of Little, Brown tried to drum up some interest in the spring list by promising that two of the firm's forthcoming novels would be suitably "erotic," rival publishers like E.P. Dutton and the New York Times Book Company let it be known that they were in the market for "erotica" (Dutton was also keeping a lazy eye out for books of "permanent literary value"), and the funsters at Dell announced plans to publish not one, or two, but *eight* "sensual adventures." (The *Washington Post* suggested that the series constituted "amazingly racy fare" for the house of Dell, but an editor at the firm set things straight: "Have you read our Candlelight Ecstasy Books recently?") Simon and Schuster hit the racks with a gigantic picture book that illustrated "the eroticism of the human figure" from the early years of the century "to the sexuality found in popular magazines today" (for which read, "500 shots of naked ladies for only $24.95"), and Penguin Books fought back with *The Nude Male*, which featured "artistic" representations of sodomy, masturbation, and oral sexual activity, coupled with a single-minded text from the pen of a feminist English professor: "In his own fantasy, in the fantasy of others, a man *is* his genitals." Bantam Books was offering interchangeable volumes of uncompromising pornography signed only by "Anonymous," CBS's Fawcett Books began issuing a series of "suggestive romances" ("bodice-rippers," according to the knowledgeable *New York Times*), and the Barnes and Noble Sales Annex brought honor to the parent firm by advertising such beloved "Classics In Erotica" as *Dirty Movies, Oragentalism* (sic), *Nude 1925* ("100 female nude postcards"), *The Love of Two Women* ("over 100 full-color photos"), *Sexual Secrets* ("600 illustrations"), *Emmanuele* ("an unrestrained erotic novel"), and *Man With A Maid* ("he lures first a young virgin, then her maid and others into the mad room of an asylum—replete with iron rings—for his own sadistic pleasures")—not to mention such "best bets for Christmas" as *Sexual Excitement, The Joy of Sex, The Joy of Gay Sex*, and (lest the company be accused of favoritism) *The Joy of Lesbian Sex*: "These popular handy-sized books make great stocking stuffers!" "Our goal," explained the stocking-stuffers at the Annex, "is to sell the finest books in the world at the lowest possible prices. Ask about us at your local school or public library."

Sad to say, the Barnes and Noble Sales Annex wasn't the only literary outfit with a marked interest in the local schools. The Macmillan Publishing Company of New York—still a member of the Children's Book Council, still bearing the proud name of a bookman who was, in the words of his biographer, "impressed with the dignity of his craft, and of its value to humanity," and "anxious that it should suffer no shame or diminution through him"—the Macmillan Publishing Company, we say, tried to get a handle on the next generation of readers by sponsoring the work of still another Californian "sex authority" who went around asking hundreds of inoffensive fifteen- and sixteen-year-old boys whether they would want "to kiss a girl's vagina," and whether they would like girls "to kiss your penis" on "the first or second date" or at some later time. No option was provided on the questionnaire for those bewildered children who didn't share Macmillan's specialized literary interests at all, but even so a sizeable percentage of the young respondents answered "Never" to those and similar questions (though it was not recorded whether or not they went on to suggest that the House of Macmillan could take its creepy old Sex Authority and go jump in the Hudson with him).

The competition was rough, but finally Random House—also a member of the Children's Book Council, and "a great publishing house," in the words of its own hucksters—came rolling out of the bog on East 50th Street with the most notorious and most repulsive volume of all, an embarrassingly breathless guide to "teenage sex" written and illustrated by a "collective" of "sexuality" experts who provided pages of excruciatingly detailed instructions in the most pleasurable methods of sexual self-abuse, and sneered at children who were reluctant to lick one another's genitals ("you don't have to worry about 'dirtiness,' " whined the representatives of the Great Publishing House). The middle-aged specialists in young lust from Mr. Cerf's old firm scaled new intellectual heights by assembling a list of twenty-four slang expressions for the publishing community's favorite portion of the male anatomy, and ordering boys and girls to practice saying the words out loud (after all, the kids would be members of the reading public some day). No self-respecting adolescent would have been caught dead with the shrill little sexbook—it was an old man's book, and not a very nice old man's book at that—and even the greasiest troublemaker in the back row would have balked at the idea of compiling a list of all the dirty words he knew, but the whole bizarre project must have seemed awfully exciting to various greybeards in certain airless editorial offices on East 50th Street, greybeards who were presiding over the destruction of still another bookselling reputation.

Such was the grotesque mood of the twisted age, an unprecedented age in which the most fortunate members of the adult generations set out—coolly, deliberately, and with ill-concealed pleasure and even excitement— to make life a hell for the members of the youngest generations. On and on they trudged, going from schools to seminars to booksellers' conventions, asking other people's children where they would most like to be licked, telling other people's children where to thrust their young fingers, ordering other people's children to chant the words that had seemed so daring at the latest Sexuality Conference. What does it feel like when you do that, Johnny? Have you tried this yet, Susie? Look at *these* pictures, children. Wouldn't you like to do *that* to someone? We're from Macmillan and we've come to ask you some questions, we're from Random House and we've come to give you some lessons, we're from the Times Book Company and we have some pictures we want you to look at.... On and on they trudged, their ghastly televised smiles illuminating the skull of their whorish culture, these last sad representatives of the Western intelligentsia, these pathetic and interchangeable young-old editors and sex therapists and publishing executives—the viscous sediment of the ancient literary community, the final residue of the lord of languages, all that was left of Shakespeare's fire.

If you would blame someone for what was done to the children in the most wretched of centuries, blame these professional bookmen, who were to have been the guardians of their civilization, and became its assassins instead. And if the surviving executives gaze at you with hurt eyes and tell you that they were merely Reflecting A Sordid Culture, tell them that they weren't hired to be mirrors of all that was sordid in man, but to be protectors of all that was fine. Blame these publishers and the writers they championed—not because they were the worst among us, but because they should have been the best, because they should have constituted civilization's first line of defense. Blame them because they went over to the enemies of humanity, blame them because they betrayed their trust, because they abandoned their posts in time of war, because they loved money more than life.

Did the leading lights of the cultural establishment ever really understand the true nature of the profitable beast they had embraced in the name of intellectual freedom? It's hard to say. It had all happened so gradually in one sense, and so quickly in another. Some of the more aggressive crusaders, like the former editor in chief of Putnam's (William Targ), had a personal interest in the affair ("*Screw* is the greatest buy in porno anywhere"), but other tolerant souls had more convoluted attitudes: "Because pornography is so accessible, the rest of the arts can wipe their brows and say, 'Whew, we don't have to have as much explicit nudity and intercourse,'" explained the former director of the Metropolitan Museum. "It permits the arts to be more exalted."

In more serious times, the suggestion that genuine art

might adjust the degree of its exaltation to the quantity of available pornography would have boggled every mind worth boggling, just as the assumption that art might ever encompass "explicit nudity and intercourse" (with the emphasis on "explicit") would have been howled out of the museum, on the very elementary grounds that art (and especially written art) deals not with explicit things, but with the implications and the consequences of explicit things. But then, these were not serious times, and genuine art just wasn't in the ball park, saleswise. On the contrary, it was a time when one of the largest bookstore chains in the country was more than happy to make room on its shelves for a series of narratives from Playboy Press that were so typical that they had variations instead of titles (*Christina's Ecstasy, Christina's Desire, Christina's Passion*, etc.), a time when the annual catalog of one of the oldest and most respected chains in the Midwest contained advertisements for volumes of "Oriental Erotic Art" (one hundred and sixty-eight—count 'em, one hundred and sixty-eight—illustrations), and for "pillow books," which were "erotic manuals celebrating sexual union" ("the stuff dreams are made on"). The venerable firm was eager to share both the credit and the literary experience: "If this year's catalog is outstanding—and we believe it is—it is because of the standards you have helped us to set.... Since many of the pieces displayed are not available elsewhere, we suggest that you keep it as a handy reference for the coming holidays or for any special occasion, including those times when you feel like indulging yourself."

Even the dear old Book-of-the-Month Club was

splashing about like a ghost of its former self, offering two lovely Book Credits to any excessively loyal subscriber who would accept delivery of Club choices like *Becoming Orgasmic* and *Sexual Loving*. "Sexual anatomy, sexual fantasies, acts and positions, orgasm, oral and anal sex," whispered the Club, not forgetting the clincher: "discussed in detail." For the children of the house the Club could recommend an inexpensive piece of merchandise from the author of *The Joy of Sex*: "talks candidly about such topics as the uses"—and oh yes, "the meaning"—"of sex, masturbation, homosexuality," chortled the boys from BOMC, remembering just in time to throw in the obligatory twitter about being "responsible, considerate and caring" (you know, like in *The Joy of Sex*). Introduce *your* child to the World of Books this Holiday Season: "Illustrations." In fact the Club was hyping the merchandise with an illustration of its own, a photo of two very young adolescents cuddling, and it was just about the most adorable thing that certain literati had ever seen. "We think children should begin with the best," explained the Club's blurb writers later, adding (in a different context) that the Club was only interested in "new books that surprise and delight us with their freshness, their grace, their importance, their vision of life." But the Chairman of the Board had summarized the situation more succinctly, back in 1976: "The Club's system of keeping readers from missing the best new books...has profoundly affected the cultural life of a nation."

It was the oddest of times, a time when *Playboy* magazine was printing photographs of—we swear it—nude literary agents, a time when the newspaper of

record in the nation's capital was reprinting those photographs, a time when one of the larger bookstore
chains on the East Coast could and did take out full-
page advertisements in various literary supplements in
order to push a volume dedicated to the proposition
that readers should—sorry—"orgasm more frequently."
Worse, it was a time when literary supplements were
prepared to tolerate and even welcome those advertisements, advertisements that included a pep talk from the
leering author: "You don't need to be inhibited by
negatives, limited by punishing old dogmas, or chained
by your fear-ridden past anymore.... You can maximize
your own excitement!"

As so often before, professional book reviewers of the
middle class had been among the very first to throw out
their punishing old dogmas and fear-ridden pasts, and
along about Christmastime Walter Clemons of *Newsweek* had maximized his literary excitement to such an
extent that he found himself recommending one
"unusually handsome and thoughtful volume" as a
Christmas gift because it encompassed "the frankly
erotic along with the functionally anatomical and
[ugh] the chastely aesthetic," and another (which featured photographs of nude and unsuspecting celebri-
ties) because it was "good nasty fun." Women might be
"ashamed" to buy the book, said Mr. Clemons, shrug-
ging his Hemingway-like shoulders, but "nobody will
resist greedily turning its pages."

If it was an order, it certainly wasn't going to be
disobeyed in the literary basement of *People* magazine,
where the crew had just gone ape over an "extremely
nasty little book" by one of America's supremely nasty

little writers, Robert Coover. Mr. Coover, who was best
known for a batch of narratives in which very graphic
and very bad things happened to naked little girls, had
"one of the most original imaginations in contemporary literature," according to *People*, but nobody wanted
to check to make sure (after all, Wilfrid Sheed had once
said that Mr. Coover "added to our stock of benign
legends," and that sounded pretty scary).

The novelist Scott Spencer was much more talented
and considerably less offensive than Mr. Coover, but he
attracted similar wails of critical ecstasy. Larry Swindell of the *Village Voice* thought that "the sex" in Mr.
Spencer's latest book was really quite, "quite marvelous." Also "essential," of course, always "essential":
why if it hadn't been *essential*, Mr. Swindell wouldn't
have given it a second glance, you may be sure of *that*.
But seeing as how it *was* essential, Mr. Swindell didn't
mind saying that there were, um, "several passages of
combustible, pulsating activity." What was merely the
predictable jerk of a tired old knee at the *Village Voice*
was something much more embarrassing at the *Chicago Sun-Times*, where poor Alice Adams was trying to
keep up with the boys: "The sexual passages are absolutely original," she shouted. "Brilliant," she gasped. It
was a good thing she'd managed to get all that out, too,
because when it came time for Knopf and the Book-of-
the-Month Club to put together some ads hyping Mr.
Spencer's pulsating book, both of the firms just happened to single out the reviewers' remarks about the
Sexual Passages for quotation. And there Ms. Adams
was, right up there in the advertisements with Mr.
Swindell, the two of them doing the ancient Chant of

the Essential Sexual Passage (Christopher Lehmann-Haupt was there too, shouting something about how he had "devoured" the book).

Not surprisingly, the disco daddies from *Playboy* were beginning to feel a bit miffed: after all, it had been their boat to begin with, and now they could hardly find a place to sit down. The Daddies grabbed a new novel by James Baldwin and started moving to the antediluvian beat: "Perversities of sexuality (both hetero and homo) are explored to the fullest. There is incest, prostitution, rape, endless horror and an equal dose of fervent passion," said *Playboy*. Good old Jimmy Baldwin: "He treats all these things with greater love and more spontaneous poetry than ever before."

But *Playboy* was beginning to sound a bit unimaginative, in an era when a very respectable and very down-to-earth critic like Peter Prescott could reveal in a very middle-class magazine like *Newsweek* that he liked Joyce Carol Oates for her unremarkable ability to write "as well about teen-age eroticism as about middle-aged lust." "I enjoyed all of the stories," sighed Mr. Prescott, who seemed especially keen on the ones about Middle-aged Lust (one in particular, "Jung would have enjoyed"). And even that was mild stuff, coming from a guy who had just issued a set of buzzing guidelines to facilitate the production of really good perversity: "True perversity, of the sort that *Lolita* and *The Story of O* afforded, must make the reader shudder in recognition. It requires of its author such an obsessive concentration that all elements of his story are transformed by the corruption at its core: the world must be made new again, just as it is in every good novel."

But time was running out: the boat was being lowered over the side, and the former literati had begun to fight with one another over the few remaining spaces.

Among the most ambitious (and eccentric) of the applicants was one of the American correspondents for the *New Statesman*, Claudia Wright. Ms. Wright began one of her book reviews by announcing that she'd "once had a lover" who'd achieved "internal ecstasy" by pelting the reviewer's naked form with stale candy. "What is unforgettable," insisted the lady from the *New Statesman*, "is the surprising 'plupp' sound, which a chocolate cherry liqueur makes upon diving from its paisley camouflage to strike the nether flesh of the female body, momentarily positioned by"—well, she went on plupping, so to speak. None of this had much to do with the book in question, of course—or with literature in general, for that matter—but it did help to pass the time while waiting for the flood.

It also helped to draw attention away from the efforts of one Madeline Gray, who was the author of a new biography of Margaret Sanger. Ms. Gray was reviewing another new biography of Havelock Ellis (for the *Washington Post*'s *Book World*), and not so incidentally reminiscing about the time she'd paid a surprise visit to the ratty old sexologist. "He surprised me by asking if I wanted to stay over with him. What really was he asking?" "Though no innocent," said Ms. Gray hurriedly, "I was afraid to find out.... What a mistake it was to refuse that invitation!" The determinedly world-weary Ellis follower wanted all book fans to share her disappointment: "The offer was never repeated. And if I

had taken it up I might have been able to help solve one
of the chief Ellis mysteries: Was he or was he not capable of normal sexual intercourse?'' At this point Ms.
Gray seemed to forget where she was and there was a lot
of disconnected chatter about "caressing naked bodies"
and—inevitably—"mutual masturbation," all of which
came together in one glorious intellectual proposition:
"Seminal emissions also include at least partial erec-
tions," thundered the scholarly Ms. Gray, and not a
voice was raised in opposition. But then, Doris Grumbach had already paid traditional tribute to the late Mr.
Ellis's "seminal work," which had "described" the
"non-evil, non-sinful nature" of "masturbation,"
"homosexuality," and all the rest of the elements in the
Grumbachian literary lexicon. (Predictably, Ms.
Grumbach liked the new biography of the old lecher
because it was, Like All Good Biographies, "unjudg-
mental.") As for Ms. Gray, it was her considered opinion that the "essential quality" of Havelock Ellis was
"radiance": "I am one of those who will never forget,"
she concluded girlishly (well, no wonder).

Gail Godwin tried to get into the increasingly specialized act by saying very loudly that John Hawkes's new
novel of "a repressed man being educated into passion
by a prisonful of unleashed women" made *her* "shudder
and nod 'yes' in alternate waves," but the poor girl
didn't stand a chance: her feeble shudders were easily
brushed aside by one Leonore Fleischer, who was the
author of a weekly column all about the wonderful
world of Publishing. Ms. Fleischer had been at a literary
party, "goggling," for some reason, at the child actress
Brooke Shields, when all of a sudden someone named

Gael Greene (who "writes about food as though it were sex and about sex as though it were food") showed up with her "sensational new boyfriend." Well, of course our Leonore was just mad to know what dear Gael was *doing* with herself these days, and so *Gael* said that she was working on something called *The Sexual Archives of Barney Kincaid*, and also doing a "treatment" of a year in the life of her boyfriend, who just happened to be a very very well-known "ex-porno star." And so Leonore asked the question that everybody in the whole literary community was asking, which was, how had the lucky couple found each other? Well, you know Gael—the first time she saw that gorgeous hunk, "it was like meeting Rilke at dinner," and the rest was just You Know. And so *Leonore* said that Gael and her Ex-porno Star were now "living and working together," and all in all it was just the most madly literary column you could imagine, what with all that high-class talk about Rilke and terribly famous porno stars and all.

By the time the sewing club had managed to establish its interest in the Important Subject, all was pandemonium. Poor Ms. Fleischer was lost in the confusion, but survivors reported seeing Ms. Greene over at *Time* magazine, where she was waving an ice-cream cone in the air and shouting something about how she couldn't *trust* people who didn't eat ice-cream, because they were the same people who "slept in pajamas" and "kissed with their mouths closed." It was all a little indistinct, but the clear implication was that sex novelists who wrote for *Time* magazine were the sort of people who never slept in pajamas, always kissed with their mouths open, and wanted the world to know about it. Which was just what we've been trying to say, in a way.

What happened to Ms. Greene and her ice-cream cone is anyone's guess; but she and her ilk will be remembered wherever men and women gather together to sing those two grand hymns of praise to the American literary community, "Yes, We Have No Pajamas," and that heart-wrenching old favorite, "They Kissed With Their Mouths Open."

Many fine old reputations were lost that day. Even the proud old firm of Alfred A. Knopf (which had once published the books of Thomas Mann and Walter de la Mare and Willa Cather and Ivy Compton-Burnett and E.M. Forster and Dag Hammarskjöld) found itself rolling drunkenly around on the lower decks, offering one more "new cultural interpretation of male sexuality" to any poor sucker who would hand over twenty bucks for a four-pound volume of erotic anecdotes assembled by an ex-model named Shere Hite. According to *Time* magazine, "raunchy pictures" of the distinguished author had somehow "turned up" in skin magazines like *Oui* and *Hustler*—not at all the sort of thing that used to happen to Ivy Compton-Burnett or Dag Hammarskjöld. "Masturbation," promised the House of Knopf; "foreplay...fellatio...anal stimulation." The Book-of-the-Month Club joined in, even going so far as to bombard its innocent subscribers with special little postage-paid *Hite* order forms. "This order will be handled by a special department," mumbled the Club's agents. We bet.

From the bowels of the doomed ship came a single—

and an honorable—gasp of horror. *"The Hite Report on Male Sexuality* is trash,"* wrote the critic Jonathan Yardley, "and it is appalling to see such a book being produced by the most respected publishing firm in the country."

But the most respected publishing firm in the country was a thing of the past. Compton-Burnett had long ago given way to *The Book of Nude Photography*; Forster had been replaced by volumes of "honestly explicit" paintings of sexual activity aimed at "primary school children"; and Mann had been abandoned in favor of (in the words of Alfred A. Knopf himself) the "tremendously profitable" John Updike. *The Hite Report* was merely the final shame at the end of a long, long road. "This book will radically alter the perceptions of American readers," shrieked the strippers from Knopf; and a grateful nation bowed its head, as if to say, "Thanks, guys, we love you too."

"Normal human vulgarity" (as one of the *Washington Post*'s senior essayists referred to it) is one of the minor vices, and the academic and literary vulgarians were not evil folk. On the contrary: they were, on the whole, a fundamentally decent and well-intentioned lot, the sort of people who would never have behaved at home as they were so pleased to behave in print.

And that was precisely the problem. In a secure intellectual climate, people will not do in print what they might do at home. Just as a public snicker from an otherwise civilized soul is often a sign of social embarrassment, a verbal and spiritual vulgarity that flourishes in the midst of silver and refinement and erudition is usually a symptom—and a source—of intellectual fear and moral uncertainty. There is a Roman saying from the first century: "When the truth cannot be clearly made out, what is false is increased through fear." So it is that minor literary and spiritual vices that develop in the flustered pursuit of elusive trends or transient popularity or new subscriptions do not always remain minor: any one of them is potentially disastrous, because all of them proceed from ethical and intellectual timidity, which always proceeds from dishonesty. "In morals," said the art historian Mrs. Jameson, "what begins in fear usually ends in wickedness. Fear, either as a principle or as a motive, is the beginning of all evil." By the same token, habitual vulgarity—in an individual or a literary establishment or a people—is extraordinarily unhealthy, because it mocks the things of the spirit, and slowly squeezes out all serious thought, all fruitful discourse, and all genuine sentiment.

In the end, that is why widespread ignorance of the verities, literary or other, is so dangerous: because it leads to fakery and to vulgar bravado, which lead to fear of exposure, which leads to intellectual hysteria, which can smother the cultural and sometimes the physical life of a civilization.

Chapter XV

Phenomena of Social Change

People to whom cruelty was repellent were acquiescing in the ridiculous notion that the more one dwelled on beastliness, the nicer and more liberated one became. Men and women who found self-conscious absurdity boring after the first startling ten minutes, were learning to sit through the stuff patiently, resisting the temptation to leave at the end of the first interval. Kindly people had learned to titter, though with some queasiness in their souls, at little magazines devoted entirely to a callow variety of cruelty and smut.... Parents were abrogating all moral responsibility out of fear that their sons and their daughters would despise them; and when they trimmed their thoughts and their words to that end, the sons and daughters grew up to despise them much more.

—Pamela Hansford Johnson

Social misfits who were unhappy with the cultural vision of the House of Knopf—or who were just bored by the whole Important Subject—could always hop across the literary wreckage to the offices of the National Endowment for the Humanities, where the resident humanists were using some spare tax revenue to fund a dramatization of the "thought'" of the radical historian Michel Foucault, complete with "such social-change phenomena as a medieval torture session, prison riots, and gay liberation and radic-lib political demonstrations." The *Washington Star* was ever so impressed: "Have you ever *heard* anyone being drawn and quartered?" Everybody laughed nervously and said that No, they *hadn't*, actually, but boy they sure would *like* to sometime, being humanists and all. Why, just the thought of it got everybody so excited that they all scampered out into the backyard to look for some more social-change phenomena.

There was a promising little pocket of the stuff over at the headquarters of National Public Radio, where the guardians of the nation's airwaves were preparing some unusually precious advertisements featuring quotations from a novelist who had built his career on the exploitation of kinky violence (right, John Irving), and there was a somewhat noisier deposit just next door at the Corporation for Public Broadcasting, where the kids were trying to humanize the public sector by funding some radio programs about "a new art form struggling to reach your ears—Punk Rock and New Wave"; but everybody agreed that the most pitiful bleats of social change were to be heard in the halls of the Kennedy Center for the Performing Arts, where the star of the disco movie *Saturday Night Fever* had just been appointed to the Artists' Committee, presumably on the theory that in the era of Social Change, one Artist could disco as well as another. The handwriting was all over the walls, the community elders were moving to the beat of a superannuated drummer, and it was only a matter of time before the swingers at the "National Cultural Center" caught up with 1965 and decided it was time to expose their charges—the People, God bless 'em—to a sadomasochistic disco version of John Webster's tragedy of 1612, *The White Devil*.

Now, when *The White Devil* was first performed before James I, it was a noble religious allegory, and it stayed that way for almost four centuries, until it was mugged by the Kennedy Center; after which it was "youth-oriented," and therefore "exploding with lust and cruelty" (also "drugs, music, and sexual display"). The new producers didn't *call* it a mugging, of course: they put on innocent expressions and insisted that the victim had merely "been met by a contemporary sensibility," which had left it reflecting "the images of 'Punk Rock' and the Manson Murders," and anyway they hadn't even been in the neighborhood at the time, okay? In any case they were much too excited to talk about the accident: "nudity and violence" were being "confronted directly," so to speak, "rather than merely implied," and, oh my goodness, the whole quivering mass of religious tragedy was suddenly "pulsating with the blare of rock music, the look of bizarre fashion and design," not to mention the "shocking senselessness of ritual murder," and of course "the forbidden erotic appeal of the pornographic imagination," and all in all the pure *culture* of it was just Too Much, but you really hadda be there to get into it. Like the whole play sort of exploited the "extravagant cultural images that surround us," you know, and we mean it was about as Humanistic as you could *get*, without actually taking off all your clothes and being Senselessly and Ritually Murdered, and hey Oh Wow Oh Wow wouldn't *that* be a kicky social-change phenomena?

And then somebody said Hey you guys wouldn't old Jack Kroll of *Newsweek* really freak out on *this* one, so the Expedition for Social-Change Phenomena went charging up to New York Town to tell Mr. Kroll the good news.

They should have known that Mr. Kroll wouldn't be interested. He was through with the sensibility of 1965: he'd moved all the way up to 1969, and he had in his eager little hands a ten-year-old atrocity by a German named Hildesheimer. It was a play—an unusually bad play—called *Mary Stuart*; but it "blew a raspberry at Schiller's idealistic treatment of the same theme," so of course Mr. Kroll couldn't get enough of it. "Hildesheimer gives us not high-flown tragedy but a sordid farce whose bitter hilarity is oddly bracing," said the critic, not bothering to hide the snicker. The play was "savagely sardonic," and there was a whole lot of very familiar "ironic wit," also a "vitriolic view of the hypocrisies of power." Mr. Kroll summarized the excitement in his own words, the musty old words he'd used so many times before: "Mary's doctor and apothecary get her stoned on some sixteenth-century version of Valium. Her French attendant makes a homosexual pass at the young assistant executioner. While dressing [the Queen],

her maid is casually mounted from behind by a lustful
lackey. Calling for her beloved pet dogs, the spaced-out
Mary doesn't notice that the poor canines have been
killed and stuffed. As the dread moment nears, the
courtiers jostle, fight, and even murder one another in
their fevered rush to''—but never mind. It is enough to
note that the twenty-eight-year-old who'd directed the
Raspberry was one more in the long line of Mr. Kroll's
"big talents of the future," primarily because his actors
got "right down in the Elizabethan dirt" where Mr.
Kroll could get a good look at them.

And indeed, that was the driving force behind the
whole movement for Social-Change Phenomena: the
desire—nay, the primitive instinct—to "blow a raspberry" at every man, woman, and child who'd ever
towered above the Krolls and the Doctorows and the
Capotes and the Styrons and the Updikes and the Kaels
and all the rest of the miserable children of despair. The
kids knew, towards the end, that they were going down
to particularly ignominious defeat, they could already
smell the dirt and the mud and the historical dust; but as
long as there was any influence left to them at all, they
would continue to heave the ancient mudpies at the
ankles of all the frustrating artists who seemed to know
where they were going and what they were doing, at all
the quiet souls who could direct instinct with reason
and control confusion with purpose, at all the people
who seemed to grasp those vast truths that the kids
down below could never grasp. The mudpies were the
eternal spoor of terror and resentment, and they were
aimed at the past and at the future, at progress and
understanding, at kindness and harmony and virtue

and happiness and purpose; but most of all they were aimed at the concept of maturity, at the social (and therefore, in this context, the artistic) responsibilities of adulthood itself. They were aimed, in other words, at the grownups: at the only class that might have been able to lend a hand, at the only class that could have reached down and lifted the kids up out of the pseudo-Elizabethan mud and put them back on their feet. And that was the little sordid secret of the cultural collapse of the twentieth century: the kids liked it down there. They were content, molding their traditional pies of social-change phenomena, and they didn't ever want to stand up again.

What the kids did want—and what they wanted with mounting fervor, as their numbers and their audiences decreased—was attention. "It is with narrow-souled people as with narrow-necked bottles," said Pope: "the less they have in them, the more noise they make in pouring it out." In those final hours, the good news was that the bottles were almost empty; the bad news was that the noise had become almost intolerable.

Some of the most unsettling gurgles were to be heard over at the *New York Times Book Review*, where the fellows at the front desk had just hired Edmund White, the proud co-author of *The Joy of Gay Sex*, to write an exhaustive description of—wait for it—the Spiritual Quest of Christopher Isherwood. Now, it can be revealed, after a furtive bit of shy-making research, that *The Joy of Gay Sex* is a profusely illustrated, rigorously porno-graphic piece of the very hardest core, not to be confused with such everyday pablum as *The Joy of Sex* or even *The Joy of Lesbian Sex*; and when you permit the leading authority on Fun Things You Can Do To Strange Boys With Your Fist to compose an essay about the implications of Indian theology, you are going to get exactly what you deserve, and the *New York Times* got it: "If I had to propose a candidate for canonization, Isherwood...would get my vote," whispered the joyous reviewer. Which didn't come as an enormous shock to those members of the congregation who had been paying close attention to Saint Christopher's own latest sermon: "Now the innocent lust which had fired all that ass grabbing, arm twisting, sparring and wrestling half naked in the changing room could come out stark naked into the open without shame and be gratified in full. What excited Christopher most, a struggle which turned into a sex act, seemed perfectly natural to these German boys; indeed, it excited them too.... Maybe, also, such mildly sadistic play was a characteristic of German sensuality; many of them liked to be beaten, not too hard, with a belt strap," and blessings upon you all, my children.

Ah, the literary life, hey, Christopher? But that's the trouble with a bookish career; it is *so* likely to lead to "innocent lust," and then to "mildly sadistic play," and then to belts, and then before you know it the National Endowment for the Humanities comes along and declares your belt a National Social-Change Phenomenon, and *then* where are you?

Probably teaching creative writing at a Major American University, if you're lucky. That's what St. Christopher was doing with his spare time, during the general collapse; and that's what his determinedly joyous disciple was doing, in those odd moments when he wasn't actually sweating over *The Joy of Gay Sex* (or his other magnum opus, *States of Desire: Travels in Gay America*, which was, according to Ned Rorem, "a twenty-city investigation pursued by White, age forty, with an adolescent's horny zeal," and brought to you by Dutton, of course). Those must·have been tough years for poor Mr. White: slaving through all those long hours in the classrooms of Johns Hopkins (and other universities), teaching fresh-faced teenagers about the creative thrust of Anglo-American literature, and then having to spend even longer hours (perhaps in the Reading Room of the British Museum?) jotting down little-known hints about the safest methods of picking up stray barboys. The cry went round the scholarly community: "What a man is White! How *does* he do it? Don't we wish we could do it too!"

Professor White explained his latest research methods to a reporter from the *San Francisco Examiner*: "I had a little bar guide and I'd just go to the gay bar in town and start talking to people." It was stimulating and demanding work, but somehow the intrepid investigator found time to take a position in the great literary debate of his time: "Lesbians attack gay men's sex, which isn't really any of their business. They say gay male pornography promotes rape, or they're against promiscuity. But gay men have gone to the trouble to come out so they *can* have their own sex lives." The littlest professor wanted to make it very clear that he, for one, was not troubled by either pornography or promiscuity. What troubled *him* was—you guessed it?—the Envy that all the rest of the world had for Edmund White's fan club: "Straight men see gay men having sex with each other, and a lot of them would like to have that much sex that easily—not gay sex, straight sex. Many gay men have a lover with whom they're not faithful but also have other quickie relationships, and this is acceptable."

Well, the faculty just wasn't what it used to be. Not surprisingly, the president of Johns Hopkins was a very weary fellow in those years, the sort of fellow who could feel the ghost of Aristotle breathing down his neck: "The biggest failing in higher education today is that we fall short in exposing students to values. We don't really provide a value framework to young people who more and more are searching for it," he told *U.S. News & World Report*, averting his thoughts from the faculty lounge. The president said that when it came to transmitting values, he would like to see his faculty "focus on 18-to-22-year-old undergraduates." "Universities have to be able to restore to people some sense of coherence, and that can't be done without humanistic values," he continued, as the fresh faces set off for their morning instruction in the creative thrust of Anglo-American literature. "The failure to rally around a set of values means that universities are turning out potentially highly skilled barbarians."

And yet, in the late 1970s and early 1980s, a high academic official who paid lip service to the humanistic verities while passing out paychecks to a pack of joyous literary barbarians was not necessarily a hypocrite. On the contrary, it was one of the ironies of those years that such an official was almost certain to be an intellectually honest soul, more victim than tyrant, a potentially positive force rendered neutral by a complicated web of codes and tenures and regents and regulations. And if by simply occupying his office he appeared on occasion to lend moral sanction to spiritual barbarity—and he did—it was only because the residual intellectual shibboleths of the postwar academic and literary communities forced that sanction from him. Indeed, the true magnitude of the institutionalized anti-intellectualism of the twentieth century would be measured in future years not so much by the number of charlatans who had filled the chairs of English literature and dominated the best-seller charts, but by the number of good men and women who had been denied the opportunity to do good.

And that was the final irony: that an intellectual establishment that had dedicated itself for thirty-five years to the Nonjudgmental gods of tolerance and open-mindedness should finish as an anti-intellectual cult of intolerance, propped up and held in place by a vast network of cultural prohibitions and quasi-legal injunctions, and distinguished chiefly for its poverty of discourse and narrowness of vision.

Chapter XVI

Shipwreck

"Enough, ye slaves, and servants of the mud-gods; all this must cease! Our heart abhors all this; our soul is sick under it; God's curse is on us while this lasts. Behold, we will all die rather than that this last. Rather all die, we say..."

Thomas Carlyle

English-speaking people who had been born after the Franco-Prussian War but before the Second World War had been born into the shell of the old world—which is to say that they had been born into the remnants of human history and the apparent wreckage of all high aspiration. The ancient verities were fast being eclipsed, but they were still visible—still referred to in books and speeches and thoughts and lives, still at hand and

226

accessible to those who might wish to know them. The world was full of splendid ghosts.

Aided by those ghosts—by memories of ineluctable truths absorbed in youth—most members of the prewar generations had been able to shrug off the everlasting whimper of the mud-gods, even as that whimper had grown louder. The vast majority of healthy men and women who had been born before 1940 had never paid much attention to the antics of the increasingly isolated cultural establishment of the postwar era. The shrieking and the writhing and the bumping and the grinding and the blood and the guts that had characterized "art" in the age of Mailer had always seemed peculiarly irrelevant to actual life as it was lived by real people: even in 1980, nobody knew anybody who actually *read* John Updike or Henry Miller on a regular basis, nobody knew anybody who tried to live his or her life according to principles proposed by manic literary critics who sang songs about pornographic liberations and artistic minimalism. Most good citizens who had been around for a few years remained largely indifferent to it all, and—quite properly—wouldn't have known or cared if the "cultural community" had lived or died or moved to Bombay.

But it was different for more recent arrivals. Those who had been born into the artistic and philosophical squalor of the postwar world had never known—or heard of—anything else. Many of them had embraced that squalor and called it "reality" because it had seemed to come with the sanction of their elders. They were, so to speak, the walking wounded: raised on the sickly fantasies of Capote and Vonnegut and Mailer and Roth, fed on the unhealthy diet of animalism in their schools and their theaters and their libraries and their universities. If the parents had never taken the charlatans very seriously, the sons and the daughters had: many of them had tried to base their lives and their dreams on the ugly diet of their youth, with inevitable consequences. Many would never quite realize what had hit them, and would never recover: they would live out their lives in twisted and uncomprehending resentment, a dead weight on the society for decades to come.

But some of them—especially the serious ones, the ones who matter in every generation—were beginning to realize what had been done to them, and to the civilization they might have inherited; beginning to understand how their nation's artists and thinkers had cheated and savaged humanity just when humanity had needed those artists and thinkers most desperately. The thunderous literary rebellion that was knocking at the door was in large measure a rebellion of victims—of youths who had been cheated of youth—and there was a real and extremely healthy element of righteous fury in it. The fury was healthy because it was the fury—the much-maligned fury—of high truth: the grudge the children bore was the most legitimate of grudges, and they watched the exhibitionistic suicide of the old guard with a little satisfaction and a great deal of impatience, as they waited for the moment when it would be possible for free men and women to break the rotting ties of the mud-gods and walk out into the sun again.

As the age drew to its dismal close, it became apparent that the rot was far more pervasive than anyone had previously realized, and that the panic had already begun to affect even the lowest echelons.

Esquire magazine, which had once featured the work of Evelyn Waugh and Thomas Mann, suddenly whirled completely out of control and came crashing to the floor with an eight-page analysis of—what else— masturbatory devices for ladies. "Multiple orgasms," according to *Esquire*, were a feature of the "orgasmo-centric" society. This explained everything, and nobody fell over backward when the editors contributed a small companion article of their very own, assuring *Esquire*'s remaining fans that they, The Editors, did not person-ally feel "envious" of "the vibrator's sexual success." On the contrary, the editorial bunch approved of "any acknowledgment by a female of her orgasmic possibili-ties," because The Editors, after serious consideration, had come to the conclusion that—speaking for them-selves, mind you—Sex was kind of, *you* know, kind of...oh, forget it. "We would very much like to hear your reactions to this article," sniffled the fellows, looking to their readers for some literary guidance, of which none was forthcoming.

One thing was clear enough: this was no longer even the ghost of the magazine that had declared, back in 1973, that it was determined "to avoid the more degrad-ing excesses of with-it-ness." By the end of 1980, exces-sive degradation was pretty much a way of life over at *Esquire*; and late at night, after the boys had gone to bed, some folks swore that they could hear the sad voice of the late Arnold Gingrich, the magazine's founding father: "*Esquire* stands for anything that will afford amusement to men of intelligence. We aim to keep our readers' minds 'amused,' thoughtfully, intelligently, and on a high intellectual level, much as that most civilized of modern men, Henry Adams, was 'amused' by the multiplicity of life around him." But then, Arnold Gingrich had lived and died long before the nation's bookmen had decided that Henry Adams was "a bore," so the late editor may be forgiven his naïve civility, God rest his innocent soul.

The saddest thing, for many present, was that the vibrating Esky boys had had the gall to leave the Gingrich name up on the masthead, as though its relatively distinguished shade might lend intellectual legitimacy to the orgasmocentric explorations of a dying literary periodical. On the other hand, observers noted that Gingrich's was just about the *only* recognizable literary name in the masturbatory issue of *Esquire*, and concluded that the ragged cultural community had not yet lost its ability to diagnose a terminal case of commercialism when it smelled one. True, L. Rust Hills contributed a perfectly grown-up little essay, but he was the Literary Editor and an all-around nice guy, so he pretty much had to. And then there was an article by Contributing Editor John Simon, but it couldn't have been *the* John Simon, the famous literary critic, because this character was taking time off to review the latest biography of the sexologist Havelock Ellis, and going on and on about the nature of Havelock's First Orgasm ("other than nocturnal emissions," mind you), and wondering at length whether Ellis's fondness for "watching his beloved urinate" was "more important for him than mutual masturbation" or not. "There was some crucial problem with Ellis's sexuality," said this

Mr. Simon anxiously; "it may have been premature ejaculation, or"—but we won't go on, precisely because Mr. Simon did. Anyway: "In the outback, masturbation may have loomed larger than it would have elsewhere." But surely not larger than at *Esquire*?

When a good and serious writer finds himself taking up increasingly precious space in order to inform his readers that "the most interesting part of the book is the evocation of the sex lives of Ellis and his circle," then it's time for the good and serious writer to seriously weigh the advantages and disadvantages of being a Contributing Editor. "No man can possibly improve in any company for which he has not respect enough to be under some degree of restraint," wrote Chesterfield to his doomed son.

And indeed, that was the tragedy of the time: that the best among us were made small, if only because there were so few to encourage and reward what was best. John Simon's country needed him desperately, but it did not need that lesser part of him that greeted the new year with an eerie little hymn of praise to the painter Balthus, "the least widely known giant of modern painting." As it happens, Balthus is not a very well-known giant primarily because he isn't a particularly good painter (he's not particularly bad, either), but that was neither here nor there, in John Simon's view (or mine): no, what Mr. Simon admired in the painter's work was the subject matter, the "perverse, inner vision," not to mention the "vague but evil suggestive-ness." The two visions he admired most were "the nymphets" and "the perverse scenes from childhood." "The nymphets" were "girl-children or girl-women,"

Mr. Simon wasn't quite sure which, and they were "sometimes nude, sometimes partly or wholly clad," and distinguished by "a guilty knowledge," and an "unwholesome superiority to their boy companions." Most of the canvas breasts that Mr. Simon had studied were "not fully developed," but one of Balthus's "several nubile or barely nubile companions" was painted when she was "almost overripe for an adolescent," and so forth. "When they are naked, these girls, whatever their age, display a hairless mound," revealed the critic, growing somewhat overly specific in his artistic enthusiasm; "sometimes they are in saucy slippers and socks that accentuate their nudity."

All the talk about the painter's models was beginning to get a bit embarrassing when Mr. Simon suddenly remembered where he was and decided he'd better say something about the pictures themselves. This was not so easily done, because Mr. Simon's favorite "perverse scenes" had been "deliberately underrepresented" by the dirty puritan who'd assembled the only available volume of Balthus's work. Still, Mr. Simon was able to say with authority that the paintings depicted "situations in which boys and girls, and an occasional mature woman...are involved in equivocal acts or attitudes, usually with sadomasochistic overtones." This was to be expected, mind you, if only because Balthus's brother was the shy author of *Sade, My Kinsman*, and because two of the painter's "close friends" were—in Mr. Simon's delicate phrase—"deeply involved with sadism."

One of Mr. Simon's own fave raves was a "seemingly innocent" painting in which the inevitable "provocative nymphet" had "removed an overshirt" and was sitting "in a serenely indecent pose, her skirt pulled up high on her bare legs," and that kind of thing. And if you liked that, Mr. Simon was willing to bet that you'd also share his enthusiasm for another entry, one in which a nude girl (with those "saucy socks and slippers," of course) "lies in a pose of either total abandon or"— here comes the artistic part—"victimization." The couch of the possibly victimized child had "overtones of the bath in which David's Marat was murdered," and also a "ferocious, masculine-looking governess type is opening or closing the curtains while malignly staring at the prostrate girl, whose body bulges toward her," and can't you just *see* it? There was some more of this depressing stuff, and then a quick bow in the direction of something called "painterly qualities," and then mercifully it was all over. "Balthus," concluded the aesthetic Mr. Simon, "has evoked a universe of his own—which is one of the hallmarks of true art."

It was also utter bilge, of course, and John Simon knew it, somewhere deep down inside his soul. "A universe of one's own" may indeed be one of the hallmarks of true art—"nature hath made one world, and art another," said Sir Thomas Browne, who knew about these things—but not just any old universe qualifies. It is, in other words, the quality of the universe that matters, and the quality is determined by the extent to which the art has become, in Sir Thomas's phrase, "the perfection of nature." Pictures of naked little girls undergoing sadomasochistic experiences just do not qualify. The surprising thing—and it was a final indication of the extent of the crisis—was that John Simon, of all people, should have been willing to go public with such a hideous little attack on the meaning of art and life. He would undoubtedly regret having done so, in years to come, because he was that sort of gentleman, and because he really did know (even if few others did) what Ruskin knew by instinct: that art is valuable only insofar as it expresses "the personality, activity, and living perception of a good and great human soul."

When Ruskin spoke of the work of the soul, he was not being abstract: he always meant to imply the work of the *whole* creature, proceeding from "a quick, perceptive, and eager heart perfected by the intellect, and finally dealt with by the hands, under the direct guidance of these higher powers." It is so ancient and so elementary an understanding of the nature of art and literature that a society that mislays it may only do so willfully. "If it show not the vigor, perception, and invention of a mighty human spirit, it is worthless. Worthless, I mean, as *art*; it may be precious in some other way, but as art, it is nugatory. Once let this be well understood among us, and magnificent consequences will soon follow." Once let it be forgotten, and disastrous consequences are inevitable.

Again, Pamela Hansford Johnson:

> Dr Frederick Wertham wrote to this effect: "When I see a couple of teenagers heading in my direction after dark, I hope to God that they have not seen *Bonnie and Clyde*." Of course, only a minority of people act out what they have seen (or read). But I believe a great number become desensitized by being exposed to scenes of, or ideas of, violence. I have seen the young become increasingly unshockable by the screened or staged display of

cruelty. What would it be like if they met with the real thing? Such as Hitler's public humiliation of the Jews? Crowds excitedly gathered round old Jewish victims in Vienna. They were laughing.
Are we preparing ourselves for a good laugh?

Any lingering hopes that the federal government might try to impose some last-minute order on the situation by announcing a few new literary guidelines were cruelly dispelled when the Library of Congress revealed to Americans the identity of their new National Poetry Consultant. Head Librarian Daniel Boorstin handed the honor to a fifty-five-year-old professor of English literature named Maxine Kumin. Ms. Kumin's poems "attest an art nearly invisible," according to the *Christian Science Monitor*, but "nearly" didn't begin to describe it: Ms. Kumin was, after all, the author of such lovely old folk ballads as "Sperm," "The Jesus Infection," and—what was surely everybody's sentimental favorite—"Heaven as Anus." What happy times the guardians of the American dream must have had down at Mr. Jefferson's old library, all gathered round the hearth of scholarship as they joined their blushing Poetry Consultant in joyful chorus:

> It all ends at the hole. No words may enter the house of excrement. We will meet there as the sphincter of the good Lord opens wide and He takes us all inside.

Which was just another way of saying that the dear old Literary Community was beginning to look and feel an awful lot like an artistic and intellectual Death Ship. Down in the hold, the remaining Brie was green with mold, and the last of the white wine had turned to vinegar. From London to San Francisco, from the *New Statesman* to the beleaguered *Nation*, life-jackets were being donned, discreet good-byes were being exchanged, and the bravest of the literary bourgeoisie were preparing to go underwater for an indefinite number of years. As the worst of times began to recede into the distance, despair had turned to resignation, and there was little hope.

Chapter XVII

Inquest

Considering the multitude of mortals that handle the Pen in these days, and can mostly spell, and write without glaring violations of grammar, the question naturally arises: How is it, then, that no Work proceeds from them, bearing any stamp of authenticity and permanence; of worth for more than one day? Ship-loads of Fashionable Novels, Sentimental Rhymes, Tragedies, Farces, Diaries of Travel, Tales by flood and field, are swallowed monthly into the bottomless Pool: still does the Press toil; innumerable Paper-makers, Compositors, Printers' Devils, Bookbinders, and Hawkers grown hoarse with loud proclaiming, rest not from their labour; and still, in torrents, rushes on the great array of Publications, unpausing, to their final home; and still Oblivion, like the Grave, cries, Give! Give! How is it that of all

these countless multitudes, no one can attain to
the smallest mark of excellence, or produce aught
that shall endure longer than "snow-flake on the
river," or the foam of penny-beer?

Thomas Carlyle

In later years, the blame for the wider cultural collapse
would be laid largely at the door of the literary establishment. And properly so: it was an establishment that
had never been able to see things whole, an establishment that had never been able to accept with grace one
of the most elementary and one of the most sophisticated truths of artistic virtue and human nature, which
is that an individual work of art, like an individual
character, must be considered in all its parts, and not
just in little pieces—because there are no little pieces, in
art or in nature.

It was, in other words, an establishment whose
guardians were unwilling to administer social, intellectual, or academic punishment to the joyous maker of an
ugly little guide to physical (and therefore spiritual)
promiscuity, for fear they might seem to be deploring or
even pitying any one of a hundred common conditions
of emotional, sexual, or moral insufficiency, a deplora-
tion that they were much too nice and much too confused to make. By the same token, if Christopher Isherwood could write a decent English sentence (and
Christopher Isherwood can write some of the best), then
it was not possible to reprimand Christopher for reminiscing in public about the dear dead days when he used
to cavort with German prostitutes who liked to be
beaten—"not too hard"—with a belt strap. It was an
inverted hierarchy of values born of a century of mass

education: a concept of literature and therefore of humanity within which the highest value was placed on an increasingly widespread grammatical dexterity ("talent," it was called, though it was really only literacy allied with idleness and normal variations of perspective), and the lowest importance attached to grandeur of vision or purpose or intellect. And as such, it in turn gave birth to the ignorance that saw literature as a nondiscriminatory catalog of random human behavior, rather than as a revelation and an exaltation of the larger human psychology and spirit. It was, in sum, a supremely Philistine view of both art and life, because it imagined literature where there was none, and because it saw no link between the quality of the art and the quality of the life.

And that is what we are talking about, really: linkage, or the absence of linkage. Which is of course what Thoreau was talking about when he said that there was "never an instant's truce between virtue and vice": he didn't say that there was never an instant's truce except when somebody on campus happened to have a sharp wit or a large vocabulary, in which case all axioms were off. On the contrary, art requires stricter judgments than life, because art must be more lucid in its virtue than life, or it is not art, but decoration. An intellectual community that understands the concept of artistic linkage is a community that is able to make distinctions and judgments over and above the purely aesthetic, a community capable of encouraging what is good in a work (or in an individual) without rewarding what is bad, capable of punishing the bad without destroying the good, and—most important—capable of determining when the one is so powerful that it must negate the other. And an intellectual class that lacks the capacity to make such judgments—which is to say, a class that calls everything "literature"—lives in a state of perpetual and increasing fear, not just of "elitism" (or anti-elitism, for that matter), but of various forms of intellectual, legal, and social chastisement.

And it is a justified fear: if there is nothing other than a title page to distinguish the most decorated art from the most lamentable society, then a civilization that decides to tighten up on itself—and civilizations do tighten up, from time to time—will inadvertently but necessarily tighten up on its "literature" as well, often with disastrous consequences.

By contrast, an intellectual community capable of making sound moral and philosophical judgments (in addition to aesthetic ones) is always able to maintain a line of defense against exterior threats of censorship. It is able to defend its intellectual credibility—and thus its civil authority—simply because it is prepared to banish anti-literary pretenders from the halls of the community, merely by dismissing them from serious consideration (even if they exhibit the most startling grammatical eccentricities) and relegating them to the realm of unpopular entertainment, where they are at liberty to pursue their printed interests with whatever degree of freedom the larger society's entertainment committees choose to permit. Such a community is happy, in other words, to bar the author of a barbaric little fornicatory workbook from the literary (and most other) columns of the *New York Times* and the *Washington Post*, on the grounds that his past performances in print render him unfit (pending some sign of intellectual rehabilitation) to speak with serious men and women about serious things.

Such actions are known as "editorial decisions," and they imply an intellectual and philosophical commitment on the part of the editors who make them. Of course there are always some editors—and some reviewers and readers and book dealers—who cannot bring themselves to make editorial decisions, which means that there is always a home for stray barbarians, which is as it should be; but because this subsidiary school of editors and writers and readers is no longer part of the higher community, it constitutes a lesser threat to art, which is also as it should be.

And, paradoxically, even as the higher community is reestablishing the principle of artistic exclusivity, it is also enlarging its membership, according to its habit of admitting and rewarding only the serious and the true: which is to say that it encourages the well-intentioned but defective artists (such as Isherwood) to concentrate their energies and define their purposes, in order that they may retain their literary reputations. In such fashion is the bad discouraged and the good given space to breathe, and in such fashion also are the arguments for external repression disarmed.

And finally, an intellectual community that believes in good and evil constitutes its own bulwark against Philistine intolerance, simply because its individual members tend to identify and preserve their various notions of the bad in order that they may glorify their separate visions of the good. So said the critic Willmott, not so long ago:

> Books, of which the principles are diseased or
> deformed, must be kept on the shelf of the scholar,
> as the man of science preserves monsters in
> glasses. They belong to the study of the mind's
> morbid anatomy, and ought to be accurately
> labelled. Voltaire will still be a wit, notwithstand-
> ing he is a scoffer; and we may admire the brilliant
> spots and eyes of the viper, if we acknowledge its
> venom and call it a reptile.

Whether one agrees with Willmott about the reptil-
ian characteristics of Voltaire or not is beside the point.
The point is that Voltaire is still on the shelves to be
read, and one of the reasons he is still on the shelves is
that Willmott had the interest and the courage to "label
him accurately," according to the code of Willmott. It is
as Auden said, in his essay on reading: "Some books are
undeservedly forgotten; none are undeservedly remembered."

The popular literature of an educated democracy,
like democracy itself, is not always a lovely thing in and
of itself: it is merely a means to a better end, and it is
good only to the extent that the people make it good. By
the same token, it is only as bad as the people allow
themselves to become. Which is to say that we must be
careful not to confuse our art with our politics: the
democratic societal and intellectual structure makes the
production (and the appreciation) of good art possible,
but not mandatory. Still less does that structure guaran-
tee that good art will be recognized when and if it does
appear.

It is becoming apparent that most of the well-known
books of the last thirty-five years will have been swept

up and forgotten by the turn of the century. They were, in large measure, the printed outgrowth of a particular and unrepeatable stage in the adolescence of a literary democracy, and that stage is beginning to pass into memory. Sad to say, the genuine literature of the period is likely to be forgotten as well, if only because humans are generally reluctant to paw through last week's garbage on the off chance of finding the lost penny or two. It is one of the tolls we pay on the way to genuine mass education, and it is a stiff one.

Indeed, the literature of a democracy in transition—which is to say the literature of a democracy just past the midpoint between widespread illiteracy and universal erudition—is necessarily in danger, simply because the citizens of such an adolescent democracy share just enough of the blessings of literacy to render them superficially indistinguishable from one another, so that the exceptional cannot easily be disentangled from the unexceptional, the serious not easily separated from the glib. The phrase "the reading public" used to have a very precise application: it referred to a lucky, well-educated minority—or, more specifically, to those few within that minority who truly cared for books and ideas. Now, it refers to everybody: the man or woman who is exalted by *Beyond Jogging* has the same vote as the man or woman who reads Plutarch. By the same token, as the ability to read and write and reason on an elementary level becomes more and more common, so does the tendency to read and write the honored words—words like "art" and "literature" and "good" and "bad"—without knowing what they mean. Much of the popular literature of an incompletely educated republic is like the love sonnet of a talented twelve-year-old: it may use some of the right phrases in some of the right places, but it has no understanding behind it, and signifies little but a promising fluency. Fluency can be valuable around the home, but when all the sonnets of precocious childhood are slapped between hard covers and hurled at an unsuspecting civilization, then "the severe discipline necessary for all real culture" (as Arnold described it) just doesn't stand a chance: it is as if a thousand different souls had suddenly hit upon the same word to describe a thousand different conditions, and intellectual chaos reigns.

It is only a matter of time before there is some upward seepage of the confusion: when everybody can grind out a marginally decent (or indecent) sentence, then everybody is a potential member of "the literary community." Inevitably, the false literati come to outnumber the real thinkers and writers and publishers, and all of a sudden the nongrammatical qualities of genuine art and culture—moral, intellectual, and spiritual grandeur—begin to smack suspiciously of "elitism," just as the mere ability to write at all smacked of elitism, some two centuries ago.

Thus is the stage set for trouble; and then do novelists like John Irving begin to complain in increasingly strident tones about "superliterary cliques in publishing" who "speak only to one another and not to the public," etc. "Elitists" are to the literary Philistines what grownups are to the twelve-year-old author of the love sonnet, and the Philistines want exactly what the twelve-year-old wants: praise from the grownups. Indeed, the only real difference between the old Philistines and the new is that the new ones don't want to be Philistines anymore: they want to be "artists" and "writers," or at any rate they want to be thought of as artists and writers. They require more than money and celebrity and a spot on somebody's best-seller list: they need moral and intellectual approbation as well.

It is when that approbation is not forthcoming that the shouting begins in earnest. "Ignorance and charlatanism in work of this kind are always trying to pass off their wares as excellent," said Matthew Arnold, "and to cry down criticism as the voice of an insignificant, overfastidious minority." The cries that Arnold heard will not cease in our lifetime, simply because the charlatans can never receive what they so desperately seek, the sanction and the approbation of the disciplined artist and the honest critic. And, in one sense, we ought to welcome the awful sound: for so long as we hear it, the battle is not yet over; and for so long as it continues to increase in volume, the Philistines are in retreat.

They will be back, of course, they always are. As Arnold saw the battle, in its early days in England, it was primarily a matter of numbers: "It is not that there do not exist...a number of people perfectly well able to discern what is good, in these things, from what is bad, and preferring what is good; but they are isolated, they form no powerful body of opinion, they are not strong enough to set a standard, up to which even the journeyman-work of literature must be brought, if it is to be vendible."

And yet, if there is cause for optimism in the long run, this must be its source: that small but ever-growing segment of the "reading public" that has always been, and is now, more scholarly, more interesting, more perceptive, and more thoughtful than the average writer or the average book reviewer or the average editor. These few men and women are the few who matter, in the artistic context, and these are the few who have always mattered, since the time of Pericles. They are the true literary and artistic democrats, precisely because they are the true guardians of culture; and to the extent that they cherish and preserve the highest values of art and civilization, to that extent may they claim with Arnold that

> culture seeks to do away with classes; to make the best that has been thought and known in the world current everywhere; to make all men live in an atmosphere of sweetness and light, where they may use ideas, as it uses them itself, freely— nourished, and not bound by them. This is the *social idea*; and the men of culture are the true apostles of equality.

We must believe in the existence of this democratic aristocracy of art, and we must also believe that in the very long run—which is to speak of centuries—its members make the final judgments. If we did not believe, many of us wouldn't write at all; and if we did not believe, there would be no honor in writing. Or, as E.B. White said: "Being democratic, I am content to have the majority rule in everything, it would seem, but literature."

On the day that the cultural minority becomes the literary majority, on that day will the shouting cease, and on that day will the social democracy have fulfilled its artistic promise.

Chapter XVIII

Prophecy

Properly understood, the eternal conflict does not lend itself to political or economic or even philosophical definition: it is not a confrontation between liberals and conservatives or Republicans and Democrats or stupid people and smart people, it is not a battle between sexes or races or governments or generations or cultures or rival schools of academic thought. Rather it is a battle between those who would be governed by the moral instinct, and those who would deny that instinct; between those who would obey the commands of the human spirit, and those who would still that spirit; between those who would have us be more than we are, and those who would have us be less than men.

247

In practical terms, it is the battle between those who would preserve and extend the highest values of civilization, and those who would use the tools of civilization—education and knowledge and liberty and peace—to savage those values. It is the battle between the host and the parasite, between those who seek and those who drift: the battle between those who stand for something and those who will tolerate anything, between those who speak of good and evil and those who speak of Alternative Lifestyles, between those who find happiness in the pursuit of goodness and those who become miserable in the pursuit of happiness. It is the battle between those who draw the line and those who draw no lines, between the life directed and the life merely endured: the battle between those who aim for virtue and those who wish for pleasure, between those who tame the worst within themselves and those who indulge it, between those who believe in purpose and those who believe only in freedom, between those who yield not and those who yield always.

It is the everlasting battle in which there are no truces, the battle between the smile and the leer, between innocence and sophistication, beauty and lust, truth and cynicism, love and pornography: it is the conflict between Dickens and Mailer, Michelangelo and Picasso, Augustine and Updike, Thomas Mann and *Garp*. It is the battle between substance and display, integrity and materialism, good cheer and quiet desperation, duty and hedonism; between earnestness and flippancy, the absolute and the expedient, the eternal and the ephemeral, the moral imperative and the passing whim. It is the ancient fight between the gentleman and the mob, the mother and the barbarian, the immaculate child and the old roué, the monk and the thug, the angel and the beast, the spirit and the brute: it is the war between the human and the anti-human.

One who spoke in behalf of life—an obscure English novelist named Gerald Edwards—used to say that all the bestial madness of our sick and sorry age could be traced to an epidemic of "helicopter thinking." The awkward but evocative phrase was of his own invention, and it came crashing into his conversation whenever he found himself trying to describe the attitudes and activities of twentieth-century social and literary engineers—"the helicopter men"—who looked down on fundamental human feelings from atop the slag-heap of purposeless technological advance and long-standing spiritual and aesthetic confusion. Victims of their own dark age, the gnomes of the slag-heap were nonetheless dangerous, because they looked not for deliverance—which they might have had for the asking—but for company in their misery. They were—and are today—like human spiders, spinning webs of despair, watching each new generation of victims from a distance, an unseemly lust in their eyes and in their books, dried-up little spirits behind their computers and their pens and their cameras and their plans. No, they are not fully human, these hard nut-like men and women, these half-souled progeny of liberty and equality and fraternity who despise their own brethren and their own hearts; they are something different, something twisted, something emerging after centuries of sleep, something released by ballot-box democracy, something to be pushed back beneath the rock. They are not whole, and they are not good, and they mean to do us harm. They would have us succumb to their own disease.

The problem, of course, is that half-souled helicopter men are jealous of whole-souled humans. It is always so: people who cannot see and feel what other souls can see and feel must become envious, if they are unwilling to confront—and learn from—their own differences and insufficiencies. Indeed, it is precisely because they are psychological outsiders that the helicopter men find themselves inventing derogatory phrases for those human emotions and aspirations that they cannot share: they speak in horrified tones of "conventionalism" and "romanticism"; they look on spiritual and ethical purpose and speak of "prudery"; they look on honor and call it "priggishness"; they look on purity and call it "naïveté." In the end, they turn simple human goodness into "sentimentality," and then the dirty work is done, and all men are like the hollow men. Then there is nothing left for them to envy; and then there is no more joy, and no more art; and then there is no more life.

The Irish essayist John Stewart Collis identified the common enemy in a recent biography of Thomas Carlyle, as he dismissed the lesser souls who sought to diminish the effect of Carlyle's warnings: "There are clever men, and cold men, and psychology men, who in their power to lessen what is great and sad have said, and will doubtless say again, that he exaggerated, that he over-dramatized, that he was being self-indulgent.... But to any reader who has joined us in sympathy as far as this, I would suggest that we leave such attitudes aside...."

The point is that there is a crucial distinction to be made between mere blindness, and willful self-deceit. It is because they cannot see clearly that the "clever men, and cold men, and psychology men"—the helicopter men—do not know what to do with real art, or real feeling, when they come across it in their galleries and their concert halls and their editorial offices; but it is because they do not want to see—and because they do not want others to see—that they seek to suppress real art before it can exert an influence upon the course of civilization, and incidentally reveal the depths of their own hollow confusions. This is their shame, and their curse; and it is our failure, and our tragedy.

It is the tragedy of the false cultural democracy: the democracy that flies against the law of the universe by pretending that virtue and meaning and wisdom may be obtained from the collective folly and confusion of swarms of unimpressive men. It is the tragedy of the democracy that sacrifices the possibility of excellence to the commonly-agreed-upon lie of equality: that in Florence would have paid equal tribute to Leonardo and his apprentice; that in Jerusalem would have given Jesus and Judas the same vote; that in Canterbury would have given equal time to Becket and his killers. It is the pity of the suicidal society that would murder the glory in some hearts because the heat from such glory cannot be felt in all hearts.

Go then and find some small portion of the priceless comprehension that was bequeathed to our most un-

happy century. Find just one shabby copy of *In Memo-*
riam or the *Religio Medici* or *Past and Present* or
Sesame and Lilies or the *Phaedo*: find just one slim
volume by one full and certain soul and take it home
and shut the door and give yourself up to its harmony.
Read it as if it were something more than a forgotten
song from a vanished state, read it as if your life and
your joy depended on its triumph, read it as you would
read the face of your beloved. Read it kindly, as you
would read the final confession of your truest friend,
and read it urgently, as if time were running out. And as
you draw near to the end of the book, commit yourself
to its unembarrassed splendor; and when you reach the
final pages, respond as your own spirit would have you
respond, because that—as always—will be the right
response, and you suppress it at your peril, and at the
peril of your civilization. Repress the highest human
sentiments, and you become a casualty of the anxious
age and a pawn of the helicopter men; deny your own
tears, and your secret knowledge of their source, and
you become a shell of your potential and a shame to
your fathers and a weight on your children's shoulders.

And when you have finished your book, get up and
go out and do something. Do something about a society
that would forbid you your tears and your soul; do
something about the Expert Editorial Advice that
would censor the human spirit in the name of current
trends; do something about a literary marketplace that
has no room for quiet men and women of dignity and
compassion and learning; do something about the
vendors of emptiness, about the intellectual charlatans
and the spiritless technicians and the literary exhibi-

tionists and the aimless governments and the hollow planners of a hollow future. Do something about the helicopter men.

Change them, if you can; change them gently, change them by example, change them through education. But do not be patient with them, for you have not that much time before the night; and if you cannot change them— if you cannot find some slender crack in their blindness, into which you might pour some small portion of the light of life and purity—if you cannot change them, then put them aside. Be gentle, and be kind, but strip their authority from them, and so turn them—and yourselves—back into men and women.

Oppose their deadly counsel in the name of Carlyle, and in the name of Emerson; oppose it in the name of Aquinas and Patroclus and Marcus Aurelius, and in the name of Arnold; do so for Haydn and Shakespeare and Handel and Milton, for Jeanne d'Arc and Praxiteles and Tolstoy and Hadrian, for an Arthur who may yet be and for the children who never were. Fight it in the name of a Greek who cried at Marathon or a sister born retarded, of a boy who died in the mud in 1918 or a mother who slept at Auschwitz, of a friend who wrote in the Gulag or an uncle you never knew: only fight it. Fight it in the name of living children, that they may in their time want children; because if you don't, they won't.

And if you lose sight of what we are struggling for—if the effect of your reading is transitory, and it will be— then go back. Go back to where you began: go back to Homer and Pericles, go back to Socrates and Plato, you cannot do better; and then follow that light, follow it to

Aristotle and Virgil, to Epictetus and St. Paul, to Luther and Erasmus and Maimonides of Spain. Follow it to Africa and see it in Augustine of Hippo, see it in Switzerland in Amiel, follow it to Sir Thomas More and Sir Thomas Browne, to Dante and Bishop Butler, see it even through the excesses of Alexander and Cromwell and Savonarola. Follow the light to all the great and good men and women who ever lived, and find them all gathered in the same place, all saying the same thing, all speaking with one voice.

Go back, then: go back to where we halted. Go back to the last of the great prophets. Go back especially to Carlyle, and forgive him his superficial bigotries for the certainty of his soul; go back also to Ruskin and Tennyson, and Schiller and Goethe. Go back and discover what it was that they knew, and why they cared so deeply: go back and study the temple they built with the bricks and mortar of twenty-five centuries. Go back and see how it all crashed so suddenly in 1917, because its guardians were old and tired, and because its shelter could not be extended to enough men quickly enough. And then look about you and see the efforts we have made in the long task of education and emancipation; see that as a society we now have the tools to do what we could not do a century ago, the tools with which to extend the highest values of culture and civilization into every corner of society, and throughout many continents. Go back, then, that we might once again go forward.

And if ye be uneducated and cannot read, then go and stand in the back of the hall and listen to the music, listen to Beethoven and Palestrina and Tchaikovsky and Bach, listen to the chants of the monks and the cello of Rostropovich, listen and you will remember what you are living for.

And if ye be deaf and cannot hear, then go and look at the pictures and the statues, go and look at Raphael and Titian and Michelangelo, at Myron and Praxiteles and Leonardo; go too and look at the waters and wander among the trees and look down from the hills, and you will know what you cannot know in your streets and your offices and your parking garages.

And if ye be unread and unhearing and unable to see, then think simply of those you love, and release your affection and bestow it upon man or woman, youth or child, grandparent or infant; give your love permanently and chastely, and demand no recompense, and you will have your answer and your purpose.

And if you have no human form to care for, there is no "sentimentality," but only honor and beauty, in loving beasts and gardens and memories and aspirations.

And if you have none of these felicities—if ye be unread and unseeing and unhearing and alone—then do not despise your suffering, but greet it quietly; for through it will you be restored.

Have you forgotten these things? Learn them again. The effort will not take so many years as you imagine, because the knowledge you seek is already within, awaiting reclamation. Reclaim it, then, and begin to fight: leave your televisions and your shopping malls and your food processors and your word processors, and come and claim your legacy as free-souled men and women. And when the automated thinkers begin to say that you are being "divisive" and "intolerant" and "contentious," tell them again what the creator of Tom Brown told them a century ago, that "man was sent into this earth for the express purpose of fighting—of uncompromising and unending fighting with body, intellect, spirit, against whomsoever and whatsoever causeth or maketh a lie." Tell them one more time the thing they hate to hear, tell them that "the first requisite of life is courage or manfulness, gained through conflict with evil—for without such conflict there can be no perfection of character"; and be yourself assured that "from the cradle to the grave, fighting, rightly understood, is the business, the real, highest, honestest business of every son of man."

"For we are born into a state of war; with falsehood and disease, and wrong and misery in a thousand forms lying all around us, and the voice within calling on us to take our stand as men in the eternal battle against them." So said Thomas Hughes.

If we as an intellectually militant people can keep before us the first Apollonian precept—"Know thyself"—then we will not go far wrong in our campaigns; and if we can recapture our understanding of the second precept—"Nothing in excess"—then our mistakes (and we will make mistakes) will not be grievous or irreparable, and our rehabilitation will be lasting.

And if the helicopter men buzz at you—and they always buzz, when their hive is threatened—laugh at them. If they say you want to "turn back the clock" or if they say you are "pulling down all that has been built," if they call you a "puritan" or a "radical" or a "Luddite" or a "prig," if they say you are a "hide-bound conservative" or a "dangerous rebel," if they accuse you of "elitism" or "snobbery" or "naïveté" or "moralism" or "sentimentality" or "romanticism" or "conventionalism," if they say you are trying to "impose your values on the rest of the world" or if they say you aren't doing it "the way it's always been done," if they say you "take things too seriously" and that you must "learn to adjust," if they say you are "living in the past" and "remembering a time that never was" or if they say you are "dreaming too many dreams" and "ignoring reality," laugh at them, and do your work.

They hate honest laughter, these helicopter men. They hate it for the same reason they hate old friendship and.young love, for the same reason they shrink from the breezes and the snow and the cries of the birds, for the same reason they fear forests and cathedrals and triumphant music, for the same reason they hate tradition and splendor and the silence of the night. They hate these things because these things remind them of that which they do not control, of the ineluctable incandescence of the human spirit. Though they may grind it into the earth of every continent, though it may sleep for centuries at a time, still that spirit will always show itself again, so long as men are on the planet. The enemies of man hate the spirit because they cannot kill it; and they cannot kill it because it is in them too, though they may waste a lifetime denying its voice. It is the mystery: it is the desire to be good. It is the secret knowledge that only by being good can we become joyful. It is the story of humanity, and it will continue to be the story of humanity, if we will it.

All high art is merely the vessel of the human mystery. It was Goethe who observed that all great literature has been produced during ages of intense belief, and that an age of spiritual confusion can never produce genuine art. Ruskin said much the same thing: "The art of a nation, so far as it exists, is an exponent of its ethical state. An exponent, observe, and exalting influence; but not the root or cause. You cannot paint or sing your-selves into being good men; you must be good men before you can either paint or sing, and then the colour and sound will complete in you all that is best.... No art-teaching could be of use to you, but would rather be harmful, unless it was grafted on something deeper than all art."

But it was Thomas Carlyle who first expressed the crucial truth as we would express it in the final decades of the twentieth century, in a letter written to his brother on the first day of October in 1833:

> In my heterodox heart there is yearly growing up the strangest, crabbed, one-sided persuasion, that *art* is but a reminiscence now; that for us in these days prophecy (well understood), not poetry, is the thing wanted. How can we *sing* and *paint* when we do not yet *believe* and *see*? There is some considerable truth in this; how much I have not yet fixed. Now, what, under such point of view, is all existing art and study of art?

A society that represents the culmination of twenty-five hundred years of Western culture should have been able to feed its children on something better than Nor-man Mailer. As final inheritors of the Western tradi-tion, we have been given the greatest chance for joy in all of human history, and we have almost lost it. Our children are beginning to open their eyes and look around; and when they see what they have been robbed of, and what has been done to them, they will not quickly forgive.

Let us therefore have some thunder in our anger, and let us finally clear the sullen advocates of the night from our path, so that we may yet live again as men and women were meant to live: as companions of the sun, as keepers of the light, as lovers of a larger fire. It is so simple: let us be still and listen to our souls again, and all will be well.